My Moments in Time

My Moments in Time

A Journey from Poverty to Destiny

Reinhold Preik
with Andrea Graff

Copyright © 2016 by Reinhold Preik.

Library of Congress Control Number: 2015921391
ISBN: Hardcover 978-1-5144-0779-0
Softcover 978-1-5144-0774-5
eBook 978-1-5144-0772-1

All rights reserved. No part of this book may be reproduced or transmitted in any form or by any means, electronic or mechanical, including photocopying, recording, or by any information storage and retrieval system, without permission in writing from the copyright owner.

Any people depicted in stock imagery provided by Thinkstock are models, and such images are being used for illustrative purposes only.
Certain stock imagery © Thinkstock.

Scripture quotations marked NLT are taken from the *Holy Bible, New Living Translation,* © 1996, 2004, 2007. Used by permission of Tyndale House Publishers, Inc. Carol Stream, Illinois 60188. All rights reserved. Web site

Print information available on the last page.

Rev. date: 02/05/2016

To order additional copies of this book, contact:
Xlibris
1-888-795-4274
www.Xlibris.com
Orders@Xlibris.com
725227

Contents

Acknowledgments ix
Foreword by Pastor Darryl Bellar.. xi
Introduction xv

    1 Defining Moments/*How Small Makes an Impact* 3
    2 A Country in Conflict/*How to Have Peace in Chaos* 43
    3 Finding What Matters/*How Focus Determines Future* 73
    4 You've Got to Be Sticky/*How Persistence Pays Off* 101
    5 Making Negatives Your Positives/
       How to Turn Weaknesses into Strengths........................... 147
    6 Never Regret a Step/
       How to Be Thankful for Every Season.............................. 175
    7 Hands and Feet/*How Generosity Brings Joy* 203

Afterword: Legacy: Living a Life Worth Leaving.......................... 239

*To my children: Marc, Krista,
Quentin, Austin, Erin, and Curtis.*

Acknowledgments

This book is dedicated to my children, Marc, Krista, Quentin, Austin, Erin, and Curtis, their spouses and their children whom I am so proud of. Thank you for the privilege of being your father and grandfather. I am so thankful that God blessed me with each and every one of you. Thank you for inspiring me to write this book and for encouraging me in the process. I hope it carries our story well for years to come.

To my beautiful wife, Jennifer, I want to say a special thank-you. Thank you for all the ways that you love me and have loved me throughout the years. I love you and am so grateful that we get to be on this journey together.

To my sisters, Ursula, Sigi, and Christel, thank you for your constant love, support, and encouragement throughout the years. Whether it was during tough war days, unwanted divorces, a business decision, or even the writing of this book, your encouragement has meant the world to me.

To my late mother and dad, thank you for the legacy you left behind. Thank you for teaching me invaluable life lessons that have made all the difference in my life.

To my staff at Chemcraft, thank you for standing and working by my side faithfully. What we created together was truly something remarkable, and I will forever cherish the memories we made in the process. A special thanks to Diana Hyunen and David Rogers for your loyalty in working beside me for so many years and also for your willingness to share your heart in this book.

To our partners in ministry: Jerry and Jana Lackey and our Love Botswana family, Pastor Darryl and Kara Bellar and our Journey Church family, and Pastor Maureen and Rocco van der Merwe and our Downtown Christian Center family, thank you for how you have enriched our lives. Thank you for allowing us to partner with you to advance the Kingdom of God. It truly is one of the greatest honors of my life.

Foreword

Rarely do you meet someone in life who makes such an impact on you that even though you have not known them for decades, their love and acceptance causes you to feel as if you've been friends forever. This is exactly the case with Reinhold Preik. His wisdom and love for people is a product of all that he has experienced in life. Instead of allowing the challenges he's faced to foster bitterness and excuses, he took every obstacle as an opportunity to grow and become a man of God that men desire to follow.

Rein is a friend who encourages, speaks truth in love, and always leaves you wanting to become a better person. His compassion and generosity have made a difference in the lives of so many. Only eternity will tell the true impact of his life and the treasures he has stored up in heaven. He brings great glory to our Heavenly Father because he is giving his life to things that will outlive him.

Rein, thank you for believing in a young, inexperienced pastor! I love you, and I am honored to call you my friend.

—Pastor Darryl Bellar, pastor of Journey Church, Fernandina Beach, Florida

We're all given a definite amount of moments—a specific amount of time on this earth in which we have to live, love, and fulfill our God-given purpose. The catch? We don't know how many moments we're given until they're gone. I hope that my moments, written on these pages, will inspire you to make to most of your own—to live intentionally, laugh freely, love wisely, work diligently, and most of all, enjoy every single one of them.

INTRODUCTION

One of my favorite verses in the Bible is Isaiah 26:12 which says, "Lord, you establish peace for us; all that we have accomplished is really from you." I love it because it describes my life so perfectly. As a young boy growing up in East Berlin during World War II, peace was something I didn't experience much. It was something that I had to learn to find in my faith in Jesus Christ. Because I made the decision to dedicate each and every one of my moments to Him, He helped me accomplish more with them than I ever thought was possible.

The truth is, I'm just an ordinary guy. There's nothing special about me or different about my life, besides the fact that I live as if it's not my own. I know that I have been blessed because of my willingness to let God lead my life. It is He who establishes us and accomplishes His amazing works through us. I am grateful that He would use me.

I hope that as you read this book, you too are inspired to let God lead your life. If you do, He'll turn it into something more amazing than you could've ever hoped for or planned on your own.

1
How Small Makes an Impact

DEFINING MOMENTS

"Jennifer." No response. She must still be asleep. It was a long trip from Jacksonville, Florida, to Botswana, and all in two days. I figure that I might as well get up. So I sneak out quietly, even managing to fix my morning cup of coffee without waking her.

The air is surprisingly warm already, although the sun has only recently risen. I sit down and sip slowly, growing excited about the events of the day. Today is a special day. It's one of those days that, to some may seem ordinary, but to me is far beyond that. It's as if I'm standing on the outside, watching myself through a glass window, wondering how in the world I ended up here.

It's one of those days filled with moments that seem to validate every life experience you've ever had, good or bad. Then you realize that just like the potter molds the clay, you've been molded and shaped for a reason, for a moment, just like this—a moment that changes things.

Life is composed of these moments, of these small units of time that often seem insignificant. But every once in a while, one moment hits that is big enough to drastically modify the moments after it. They're what we call defining moments. Just one of them can introduce a bit of information, a person, or an event that can, in an instant, alter the entire course of a life. They can influence them for better or for worse, but without a doubt, they leave their mark.

So here I am in one of these special moments at the grand opening of the Life Center in Botswana. I am here with Love Botswana, an organization I have invested not only funding but also time and prayers into. Sitting in my chair, watching those whose lives I am privileged to help improve, I imagine how this moment isn't just my moment; it's theirs as well. It might be great for me, but it has the potential to be even greater for them.

At this center, orphaned and rescued children will receive life-building tools, which they likely would have never received without it. The whole Maun community in Botswana will have access to resources that they might have never had access to had it not been built.

This forty-thousand-square-foot building will be used for everything from the Village Church services and weddings to political meetings and school functions. Many defining moments could occur here: introductions to Christ, graduations, job trainings.

My hope is that because of this Life Center, lives would never be the same. My prayer is that they would become who they are meant to become, that they would fulfill their purpose on this earth. My desire is that this moment would set them up for a remarkable future.

My heart is filled with joy and expectation as I dream about the potentials of everyone but especially these precious children who still have many years before them.

As the sun begins to assume its spot in the morning sky, my mind slowly wanders. It drifts back to another little boy and his first life-changing moment nearly seventy-five years before.

No One Is Safe

It was in the autumn of 1943 that I encountered my first life-changing moment. It was one that I would never wish on anyone. I was going about my typical nine-year-old business, running around outside, pestering my younger sister, when all of a sudden, a strange, shrill sound pierced the air. It might have been an unfamiliar sound, but anyone, young or old, could interpret its meaning: trouble was on the way.

Sure enough, in a matter of minutes, Mother and Dad gathered my sisters and me and hurried us down to the basement, in hopes that we'd be safe there. My hands shook inside of my mother's. My knees knocked together as I rushed down the stairs. I was scared, and I didn't even know why. I heard the sharp siren penetrate the night air, but I didn't understand just how great the terror was that we were about to face.

That is, until the first firing began. As I heard the first fragments hit the ground, it's as if my eyes were opened. The bombs that fell destroyed every living thing around them. I wondered if this would continue for long, and if so, just how long it would be until I could no longer escape its destruction.

With those explosions of wood and fire also came an explosion of sorts in the heart and mind of a little boy—a little boy who had already begun dreaming of his future. In an instant, I realized that every dream my young heart had dreamt was now up for question. Something beyond my control might have more say about what my tomorrow looked like than I had.

If the air raids didn't tell the future well enough, my parents' faces did. Their frightened, tired, and worried expressions told much more than the falsely encouraging words of the leaders of the German government. No matter how hard anyone tried to be positive about the situation, it was obvious that this terrible event wasn't an accident, and that it would certainly happen again.

It was obvious to us all that from that point on, life would be different. We weren't safe. No one was. This wouldn't be the last bomb to fall. It wouldn't be the last friend we watched lose their home. It wouldn't be the last night we wondered if we would survive.

In a moment, life as we knew it had changed. In a moment, the once steady routine I thrived on was stripped away; and a new, uncertain routine was forced upon me, as it was upon every person living in Berlin at the time. Even today, some seventy years later, when I hear a siren, all the hairs on my arm stand up. It is a recurring event that is forever etched into my memory.

The air raids continued incessantly, until there was no question in my mind that our country was heading straight for disaster. It wasn't long before people were missing and before my friends' fathers stopped coming home from work. People everywhere were getting called in to fight the war. It wasn't long before schoolyard conversation turned to whose mother Russian soldiers had raped and which ones had gotten pregnant as a result. It wasn't long before my boyish idea that I was invincible was overtaken by the awareness that my life could be cut short at any given moment. It wasn't long before my once calm days, filled with hope and happiness, became tinged with the looming fear of poverty and death. The worst part was that there was absolutely nothing I could do about it.

A Beautiful Inheritance

As the months went on, the raids only got worse. Close to our home, there was an open area the government used to install a couple of searchlights. As soon as those lights came on, my sisters and I couldn't keep our eyes off of them. Mother would try to divert our attention so that we wouldn't be afraid, but her tactics never worked. We were mesmerized.

Every once in a while, an aircraft would get caught in the lights and the antiaircraft guns would start firing. When the shots hit an aircraft, the German soldiers would immediately search for the wreckage to see if there were any survivors or unexploded armaments remaining that could cause future damage to those nearby. Thankfully, not many aircrafts were hit because of the inaccuracy of firing.

Soon after the target searching and firing came the bombing, and it only got worse from there. Those raids were nothing short of terrifying, although the routine became almost second nature. Upon hearing the sirens, my entire family—my mother, dad, sister, grandparents, and me—would dart down into the basement of the house and wait for the all clear. I remember well almost falling down the stairs as I tried to move quickly, my little heart beating like a drum.

After a few minutes, the explosions and aircraft firing would stop, and we would be free to return to our living area.

The next morning, my sister Ursula and I would race outside to discover and collect the fragments that came from the exploded antiaircraft shells. It was almost as if holding those shells gave us hope in the midst of devastation. It was as if holding the British's failed attempts between our fingers gave us confidence that they wouldn't win, that they *couldn't* win.

As time went on, bombings overtook artillery firings. The moment we heard the whistling sound ahead of the bomb, we ducked and cringed, hoping and praying that it was not coming in our direction.

One day, we were visiting my dad's sister, her husband, and our cousins, who lived just outside of Berlin, when the alarm sounded. As the bombs began dropping, we panicked. We didn't know what to do!

Thankfully, Dad heard my uncle yelling for us to come to the room he was in. In the middle of this room, he rolled back the carpet to reveal stairs leading down to a secret basement. As a little boy, I was amazed at this real, live secret passage. For a moment, I almost forgot the trouble we were in! We each climbed down the ladder quickly and took our places along the hard wooden benches lined against the walls. With my eyes shut and my teeth clenched, I listened to the sound of my parents, uncle, and, aunt pleading with God to save us.

In that moment, I came to the sobering realization that it didn't matter who you were or how strong you were. Anyone could be taken. Any life could be lost. The terror you experienced upon that realization was undeniable yet at the same time unexplainable. The understanding that no one was safe hit your heart like a ton of bricks and sent your mind into a tailspin.

In the beginning, raids only occurred once in a while; but as the war went on, they came more frequently. The Americans flew during the day and the British at night. Sleep was constantly interrupted by the shrill sound of sirens wailing. Sometimes they were only drills, but most of the time they were real. And every time they were utterly horrifying.

The government soon encouraged every family to find a place to hide during the raids, other than their basements. So one day, Dad and his dad, my Opa, decided to build us a bunker. They dug a hole in the backyard at least six feet deep, with several steps leading down into it. The building process was a fairly long one. They first dug a hole large enough to fit us all in. Then they put timber across for support and covered that timber with metal molds Opa had once used for the manufacturing of concrete tiles.

Finally, on top of the molds, they placed sod and sandbags. Although safe, this bunker wasn't guaranteed to keep us out of harm's way. If a bomb exploded too close to us, the bunker would collapse and leave us buried in a hole.

With Opa, 1935

For the next few weeks, we retreated to that homemade bunker when the alarm sounded. No one enjoyed being in there, but Mother especially hated it. There were no lights inside, so it was dark; and if it rained, it got awfully wet.

Sometimes, while waiting for the all clear, we'd find Mother shaking in the corner, having a panic attack, something we children got used to in the years that followed. Although it usually took some time to calm her down, we always did. We'd remind her that regardless of the inconveniences it presented, this hideout is what kept us alive and together, so we should be grateful for it.

Following every raid, we emerged from the bunker to see whose homes were still left standing and whose had been demolished or, at best, disfigured. I'll never forget the time a bomb hit the Müller's house, which was not far down the street from us. The entire family was killed. My little heart broke as I realized that I would never get to play with my neighborhood friends again.

It was in moments like this that I wondered how much of my life I would get to live. Would I make it to see my ninth birthday? Would I become an orphan? Would I finish school? Would I get married? Questions like this—questions that should never enter the mind of a nine- or ten-year-old—flooded mine on a regular basis.

Thankfully, I had parents who had taught me to have faith for the future. In those early years, they helped my siblings and me build a foundation strong enough to withstand any problem that we would ever encounter. We might not have had much of a financial foundation to build from, but we did have a moral and spiritual one. We might not have received much of a physical inheritance from them, but the inheritance we did receive was greater than any amount of money they could've possibly given us.

The inheritance they gave was one that consisted of defining moments and special lessons that I will forever cherish, ones that have helped shape me into the man I am today.

Humble Beginnings

I grew up the eldest and only son in the family. I was "all boy," as my mother would say. I loved to be outside, playing ball, catching bugs, and doing anything physical. The funny thing is, according to the doctor, I was supposed to be a girl. My parents even had the name picked out. They had planned to call me *Renate Preik*.

A few months before my mother's due date, my aunt had a baby girl whom she named *Renate*. Mother was disheartened when she realized she needed to find a new name for her daughter so quickly . . . until she realized her daughter was really a *son*.

I was a good kid, more disciplined for my age than most. I did my best to obey, partly out of fear of mother's strictness and partly out of respect for her work ethic. I knew that she worked hard to cook, clean, and perform all the tasks that kept our household afloat. And if I forgot, Dad quickly reminded me. In the Preik home, we learned that family is a team effort, and that we all had a part to play in making things run smoothly.

My parents might not have been known as the most wealthy or prominent couple in our area, but people loved them. We had visitors often—many times twenty to thirty people at once! Dad was a jokester, always pulling pranks and making people laugh, and Mother was an incredible cook. Still, it was more than just a surface-level love that our friends had for my parents; it was a deep sense of respect.

People admired my parents for the values they lived with, which shaped my life and my sisters' lives as well. They trained us in how to treat people—friends, family, spouses, anyone we came into contact with—with honor and respect. They taught us about family, faith, and the value of hard work. They demonstrated the importance of honesty, loyalty, and sticking together throughout every season of life.

I found that with these values, *anyone* could live a meaningful life.

Of course, no parents are perfect. You know it when you're a kid, and you know it when you're an adult. But never could I have asked for parents greater than the ones that I was blessed with, and never could I have asked for an inheritance greater than the one they gave. It was one that taught us to value family, rely on faith, and live with grit.

Value Family

Family was without a doubt one of the most important aspects of my parents' lives. My mother grew up in Worms, a Southern German city quite a ways from Northeast Berlin, the busy city in which I grew up. Once my father married her, she moved to Berlin with him, and they settled there, just on the outskirts of the city.

My father, Walter Preik, and my mother, Frieda Rissberger Preik

My father's parents were from Prussia. Opa had built his own business there as a construction supervisor. Because most homes in Prussia were brick homes, he learned bricklaying and soon became one of the best in his area. Unfortunately, when Dad was a young man, Opa lost his business during a market crash. Inflation skyrocketed, and money lost all value.

Because Prussia was farm country they didn't have many homes to build to begin with. Now, in addition to the preexisting shortage of work, money was so tight that most construction was stopped or put on hold. Opa was left with little business, certainly not enough to support a family.

On the contrary, Berlin was booming, so Opa and Oma decided that is where they would move. They rented an apartment and brought along their seven kids who were still living with them at the time, including Dad. Once the kids were gone, Opa, Dad, and a few of his brothers built a two-story home for Opa and Dad to live in once it was finished. That's the house I grew up in—the home that still holds some of my fondest memories.

Mother and Dad outside of our house in East Berlin, 1932

I loved both sets of grandparents, but I grew up close to my father's, since they lived with us my entire childhood. We lived on the top floor of our house, and they lived on the bottom. I have always been incredibly grateful for Opa and Oma's presence and influence in my life. They helped me build a foundation of faith and morality that I was never able to stray from—one that has truly made all the difference in building a life of significance. My grandparents were married fifty-two years before Oma died. No one could ever doubt their love for each other. It showed all over them, every time they were together!

Mother and Dad met on a retreat with their church youth groups, and from the day they met, they were together as much as possible. Dad would ride his motorbike all the way from Berlin to Worms to see Mother every chance he got.

Mother's home situation was not a happy one, so she was ready to get out on her own. Her mother died when she was a toddler, and as in many cases, the remarriage caused friction within the family. She did not get along with her stepmother well, and that made it tough for her to stick around.

Mother and Dad dated several months before he proposed. She accepted, and they were married December of 1932 in Berlin. My mother, Frieda Johanna Rissberger, then officially became Mrs. Walter Preik at only nineteen years old.

I was the first Preik child, born August 13, 1934, in Berlin. I was a typical eldest child—responsible, hardworking, and helpful. However, I was also a typical boy, a bit rowdy, always full of energy and jokes. I loved to read, swim, and play soccer. I was still young when I discovered my "need for speed," as my father liked to say.

For about a year, I begged Dad nonstop for my own bicycle. We didn't have enough money at the time, so he just let me borrow his. I'd do my best to stretch my little legs across the middle bar, but that rarely worked, so I'd settle for putting my legs through it. Learning to ride a bike that way called for a lot of bruises, scratches, and broken fences. It took some time, but I eventually learned to ride well.

After a while, Dad was able to obtain used bikes for all of us. We'd often go riding as a family. I loved those rides more than anything else we did together.

Playing outside, 1938

Besides my immediate family, I spent a lot of time with my cousins and friends from church, who felt like family. We'd go to the lake to swim in the summer and ice skate in the winter. Mother was always concerned because the lake would rarely freeze over completely. We'd skate on the edges, acting like little daredevils as we teased the cracked ice. We kept as much as possible from her, out of fear that her caution would keep us from our fun.

In the summer of 1948, a couple of friends from church, Manfred and Gerdi, told me they were taking a two-week bicycle road trip to the Baltic along with a couple of their friends. Because it was only a few years after the war had ended, there weren't many cars on the road. You couldn't take a train, bus, or streetcar; you had to take a bicycle.

I wanted to go so badly, but I knew how strict Mother and Dad were. They said no, as I suspected, but I came up with every idea possible to convince them that I was responsible enough to go. My persistence eventually wore them down, and they agreed. My excitement was out of control.

I was about fifteen years old at the time, and these guys were all eighteen and nineteen. I felt so cool taking a trip with them. Our plan was to ride from Berlin to Ruegen, an island in the Baltic, and then to ride back.

The morning of the takeoff I had no trouble waking up. I jumped right out of bed, left a note for my parents, and sneaked out the front door quietly so that I wouldn't wake anyone. We met in front of one of my friend's houses to settle our plans before riding out. We all agreed: we would ride every day from sunup to sundown.

"How much food do we have?" Manfred asked.

"I have one loaf of bread," Gerdi answered.

"I have one too," one of the friends said.

"We . . . ummm . . . we had no extras at the house. I didn't have anything to bring," the last guy said as he looked at his feet.

The other boys were gracious with him. I felt a mixture of emotions. I felt badly for him because he seemed embarrassed, but I was also relieved because my answer would be similar. Everyone's eyes turned to me.

"I have coffee beans," I said. I tried to speak confidently, but the shakiness is my voice was evident. "We can chew on the beans to keep us awake."

To my surprise, the boys were pleased with my contribution. Coffee became precious to us on that trip, since it was a stimulant and allowed us to ride for longer. Some of them hadn't had coffee since years before the war.

As we loaded our packs and mounted our bicycles, it was decided: we'd take turns stopping at houses and asking for food. At night, some farmers would let us sleep on the hay in their barns. If they didn't tell us we could, sometimes we'd sneak in and sleep anyway. We each packed a blanket to make ourselves a little pallet on the hay bales.

That morning we took off, I never felt freer. With the wind rushing through my hair, the scenery whipping by me, and the seemingly endless road ahead of me, I felt right at home, although I would soon be miles from it. This was a true adventure, and I loved every single minute of it.

That is, until the accident. About halfway through our trip, right after we had gotten on the road for the morning, I had a little mishap. While crossing railroad tracks at a fast speed, my front wheel turned and got stuck in one of the grooves. I flipped, rolled down the tracks, and landed hard in a ditch nearby. The guys parked and ran up to me as quickly as they could. It was a bad wreck. All I could see were stars from hitting my head, but I knew the boys were there.

"Rein! Rein! Are you okay?" one boy yelled.

"Quick. Get him up!" another instructed.

They mounted me on one of their bikes and drove me slowly and carefully into the nearest town. There, I came back to my senses, as they cleaned up my cuts and bruises and worked to get my bike back in riding condition. We couldn't do it ourselves, so we asked around until we found someone who could repair it. It delayed us a day or two, but we were so shaken up that we needed that time to gain the confidence to ride again.

We made another stop on that trip, but this one had nothing to do with cuts and bruises. It was much more enjoyable than the last. On our first Sunday away from home, we decided that we wanted to go to church. We stopped at one near us and met a nice Christian family during the service. They had three daughters. (And there were three of us. What a coincidence!) They invited us to have lunch in their home, and we gratefully accepted. What a blessing to have *real* food. I can still smell the chicken in the oven, taste the buttered potatoes, and see the spread of colored vegetables. We felt like we were in Heaven!

That night, we decided it would be fun for each of us to take one of the girls on a date. We took them to a movie and out for ice cream (which postwar was really nothing more than colored ice), and we had a great time. It was a refreshing stop. The next morning, we thanked the family as they loaded us up with extra food for the way. We made it to Ruegen the following afternoon and enjoyed the beach there for a couple of days. Then we began our journey home. We had been gone for nearly two weeks when we finally saw the outline of our hometown on the horizon.

So this is why they call it the Grey City, I thought as we rode up to it.

I'd learned in school that Berlin literally means "bog" in Slavic, and I could see why it was given its name. Large swamps surrounding the city created a gray smoke that seemed to fill the entire outline of the area. By this point, my beloved city had been through so much that I felt the gray seemed even more prominent. The heaviness in the air wasn't just visible; it was tangible. The dark sadness could be felt as you walked through the streets. It was going to take some time for postwar Berlin to get back to its bustling, joyful atmosphere.

A House Full of Girls

My oldest sister, Ursula, was born February 11, 1936. She was always a beautiful girl and incredibly smart. Because we were close in age, we were always together. I felt as if it was my duty to look after her. We got into trouble together many times, usually when we let our curiosity get the best of us. One of the most memorable times was when what started as an innocent game of peekaboo ended with an unwanted trip to the ER.

Mom had told me not to play on the staircase, but my little four-year-old mind didn't understand the concept of heights just yet. Trying to escape from Ursula's sight, I dodged quickly to one side and then to the other, when all of a sudden, my foot slipped, and I fell rapidly to the bottom of the staircase. I broke into tears instantly. Mother spanked me for disobeying, but soon she was the one crying when she discovered all the blood oozing from a wound on the front of my head.

I could tell she felt just as terrible as I did as we rushed to the ER. That accident called for my first encounter with a needle, but once the stitches were out, I was right back at it, causing more trouble with my little sister.

One of Ursula and my favorite games to play was ding-dong ditch. At my command, we'd take off, ringing as many of our neighbors' doorbells as we could before we got caught. Usually, we'd make it to about twenty houses! No one ever caught us. We'd chuckle when we'd hear the mothers complaining to one another.

"Someone has been ringing my doorbell again."

"Mine too! Have you caught them yet?"

"Nope. I have no idea who it is!"

Ursula and I would play it off, casting a knowing glance at each other.

The road leading up to our house was a side road, so it was made out of sod instead of being paved. That made it easy for us to play all sorts of games. From baseball to soccer to military freeze tag, we never got tired of running around! The big question always became who would get the ball when it went into the neighbors' yard. It was a well-known fact among our friends that the neighbors lacked in the sense of humor department. And Ursula and I had firsthand experience of that!

Even through the cuts, scrapes, and bruises, Ursula and I always had a fun time together. She left to take a job in for West Germany about three years after I left to Canada, but we always remained close.

With Ursula, 1939

Next came Sigi, who was born March 5, 1943. I can remember so clearly Mother coming home from the hospital after having her. Even now, I can picture her walking slowly up the stairs to bring us our new little sister. Our faces beamed with excitement. We could hardly wait to have a new baby in the house! As she got older, it became obvious that Sigi was a clown. She was little but feisty!

Christel was the baby, born after the war, on February 19, 1946. She had beautiful red hair and was incredibly sweet. Christel was innocent and talkative, which can be a dangerous combination, especially during the Communist era in East Germany. We made sure she was never told family secrets. The times were much too dangerous for little Christel to unknowingly get us into trouble.

Sigi and Christel were the best of friends and somehow always found themselves in some kind of mischief. They were little businesswomen, who loved to bring in payment of any kind, especially in the form of treats. They used to color little flyers that read, "Sigi and Christel Preik, the singing sisters, coming to your home this afternoon." Then they would dress up, traveling from door to door, singing songs they had learned in Sunday school. They'd even do little dances for extra entertainment. The neighbors loved it!

Before the Berlin Wall was built, they often crossed the border to smuggle chocolates, taffies, and sweets back to the East. Thank God they never got caught because an act like that in those days could call for serious punishment!

I got along well with all my sisters, once they came along. I felt as though I was their protector, shielding them from all harm. Being a big brother was and still is one of my most cherished roles.

> ## In Their Words
>
> *Rein was always a leader. Growing up, young boys would follow him anywhere, and they'd do anything he asked them to do. He was also extremely compassionate. I'll never forget him carrying me home after a bad fall. He is and has always been a wonderful man and brother. (Sigi Oblander, sister)*

Dad, me, Sigi, Christel, Mom, and Ursula, 1952

Spare the Rod; Spoil the Child

Discipline was a big deal in our home. Although we didn't get spankings often, when we did, they were not fun. Mother usually took care of the little stuff, and Dad, the big stuff. When we knew the paddle was coming, we always hoped Mom would be the one carrying it!

The worst punishment came from lying, something I got in trouble for a few times in my teenage years. The lies I told were nothing major, but they were lies, nonetheless. I'd tell Dad that I was going to spend the night at my cousin Günter's house, and we'd sneak out and go to the movies, a place I was not allowed to go. Without fail, one of Dad's friends would see us and make some innocent remark to him about it. They had no idea the trouble they were causing me!

When I got home, Dad would ask, "How was Günter?"

"Good." I'd reply.

"What did you guys do? Just stay at his house?"

"Yep."

Then came the stare—the one you didn't want to get. The one that made you want to repent of every wrong you had ever committed.

"Okay," I'd break down. "We went to the movies too."

Then I'd go on a rant about how all my friends went to the movies, and I couldn't understand why my parents wouldn't let me. Still, Dad would pull out the paddle; and as he spanked me, he'd remind me of why lying was a bad choice.

"Lying will get you nothing but trouble. It'll catch up to you," he'd say.

Normally Mother would be in the background yelling, "Walter! Don't spank too hard!" Although she was strict, she was also merciful. Her compassion for us shone in her eyes.

The House That Built Me

Our house was two stories, with a living area at top and a basement on the bottom. Mother, Dad, my sisters, and I lived on the top level; and Opa and Oma lived on the bottom. Although it was not a huge home, we had plenty of room for all eight of us to live comfortably. Outside, we had a garden and fruit trees, where my sisters and I would spend our summer days picking and eating the ripened fruits and vegetables.

Mother was extremely busy while we were growing up, as were most women of the time. There were no modern-day machines or appliances to help out. Food was jarred and preserved for the winter. I can only recall Mother spending money on herself in a hair salon a handful of times. Even then, it was only because she had gotten a second job cleaning a house somewhere and had some extra cash to spend.

At night, we had to sleep in thick featherbeds to stay warm because the only fire we had was in the kitchen. There was no central air or heat and no stoves, gas, or electric. It was available at the time, but it was so expensive and the times so tough, hardly anyone could afford it. I grew to dread the winter season because it was a difficult task to stay warm. Sometimes, I'd leave a glass of water beside my bed and wake up to a glass of ice the next morning!

Heating the house was a lengthy task, but we had to do it. On weekend mornings, Dad would leave early to cut branches off trees, sometimes having to travel to a forest several miles away from our house. I was about twelve or thirteen by this point, so I'd often help with this part of the job.

Right after the war, a lot of trees were cut down, so we had to settle for stumps instead of trees. The stumps had to be extracted, which was hard work and took a lot of time. We would then load the wood into a wagon and take it back to the house. Once we got the wood home, we would split it and lay it in piles to dry up.

I'll never forget one specific day of this wood searching. It was freezing, but regardless of my numb hands and aching feet, we had to gather wood. We had to keep our family warm.

I watched as Dad chopped the stumps into even smaller pieces of wood. I stood there, frozen to the bone, wanting so badly to cry and complain about the cold. But then I realized: the only way to get warm was to move. I needed to start working.

That was a defining moment for me. My attitude shifted that day, as I realized that **life can be tough, but it's always better when you're moving. It's always better when you're progressing toward a goal, toward a better life.** So I got to work.

We all pitched in with chores, usually pretty willingly, *especially* when the choice was between homework and chores. I'd take on tasks such as feeding the rabbits and chickens, turning the soil in the garden, planting and picking fruits, vegetables, and herbs, shoveling snow in the winter, and doing dishes.

During the war, I would even go stand in line for Mother at the grocery store and the butcher's shop. I would get there an hour or so before it opened, and then Mother would come a few minutes before the opening, take my place in line, and negotiate with the storeowners. I wasn't allowed to handle money or food stamps, since there was negotiation to be done. Mother laughed when her friends told her that I had stood my ground with the other women. I might have only been eight years old, but I wasn't going to let them cut in line!

Only on rare occasions, such as the times Oma and Opa were both extremely sick, would Mother stay home and send me to shop instead. I'm sure the whole time she was praying that I would come back with the right things. We didn't have any money or stamps to be wasting! A few times I finally got to the front only to hear the dreaded words, "Sorry, we are out of food." Those were the most disappointing words to hear.

My sisters had chores as well, but they were much smaller. They usually helped Mother with dinner, laundry, and with cutting and cleaning the vegetables we picked from the garden. In the summer, we harvested what had been planted and then cropped it in, storing some for the winter.

The only chore my sisters and I weren't a big fan of was laundry. We dreaded hearing that it was a "washday," but those days seemed to come around with amazing regularity. Twice a month, Mother would do the family laundry, spending two days down in the wash-kitchen. Our basement was separated into three parts: one area was for the storage of vegetables and coal, one was for canning, and one held the iron kettle and the washboard. Mother especially hated being down there all day because there were only small windows, and the room was constantly filled with steam.

Washdays started early. Dad and I would wake with the sun to bring in the wood from the backyard that we had laid out to dry. Then Dad would build a fire in the huge iron kettle. After it heated, Mother would put the clothes on to boil, soaking them in lye (homemade soap made with grease) and putting them into a big tub to scrub with a washboard. After the washing process was over, Ursula would help hang them out on the line to dry. Then they were folded and taken to the drugstore to be pressed on the big roller.

We may not have enjoyed washdays, but this simple chore taught us a great lesson over and over again: **families work together. Not only do they work together when there's a job to be done, but they also stick together when there are challenges to be faced.** Nothing would prove that more than the unthinkable hardships we were about to encounter.

Whether it was sickness, hunger, poverty, or surviving the infamous air raids of World War II and cross-country treks searching for safety, we always knew we could count on one another. Family *truly* is one of the most important parts of life. Family truly *does* matter.

Rely on Faith

Both my parents and grandparents modeled lives of faith for my sisters and me. They showed us that faith and integrity go hand in hand, that not only is someone watching *out* for you, but He is also watching *you* as well as everything that you do. We were taught that God's blessing would come as a result of the choices we made.

Throughout my entire childhood, we attended the same little Baptist church in East Berlin (that is, except for the months we were evacuated). It was located in a part of the city that was at times difficult for us to reach, since we didn't own a car, and many days didn't have bikes available.

On those Sundays, we would take a bus or streetcar. It might have been hard to get there, but it would take more than a lack of transportation for my parents to let us miss church! This congregation became a very large part of our lives. We learned valuable lessons in those services that gave us wisdom and peace, especially during the stressful times of war.

Opa and Oma were sick often. Because of the hard work they had done for so many years, they both suffered from varicose veins as well as a flesh-eating disease that caused open wounds all over their legs. They had no antibiotics and had to change their bandages at least twice a day.

Most Sundays they were not well enough to go to church with us. On those days, they would have devotions together at home. Oma also had women over for prayer meetings. Sometimes I'd hear them praying so hard it would scare me!

I could often hear Oma and Opa starting their prayers with "Danke Gott . . ." as they began the day thanking God for His many blessings. No one ever heard them complain, even though they had more than most to complain about. In fact, Oma was notorious for singing as she worked, even in the toughest of times. My grandparents were people of incredible faith.

One of my fondest memories is gathering around the table with my sisters to listen to Oma's Bible stories. She told them, not in some old-fashioned, boring way but in a way that made them come alive. When she spoke, time flew by. I couldn't keep my attention off of her. She told the stories with such detail, and as she did, a passion for Jesus shone in her eyes. With Oma around, I always looked forward to learning about Him. And those lessons definitely paid off.

The ten years that followed were extremely tumultuous years for every German family living in Berlin. Many things took place in our lives; however, my family had a peace in our hearts that many others lacked. We had the comfort that we were not alone and that God was in control.

When he first came into leadership, Hitler used the Church to his advantage. Until 1945, the Lutheran and Catholic Churches were used to further his own personal ideas. Then after the Communist socialists took over, they tried to extinguish anything relating to Christianity or any organized religion.

They were never able to extinguish the Lutheran or Catholic Churches. However, the smaller churches, especially those working to reach out to the community in our time of need, were treated badly. They were treated so badly in fact that many of them had to move underground, meeting in homes and places out of view from the Communist party members.

For years, in German schools, the Bible was taught as part of the curriculum. Once the government started shifting, they introduced us to this thought that people are purely good, that utopia was just around the corner, and that the Christian faith is an obstacle to us living in our ideal world.

These socialistic progressive ideologists changed the way we were taught. They didn't throw out the Scripture immediately for fear that people would figure out their plot and resent them for it. Their plan was much more subtle and much more dangerous. It seemed to be a form of brainwashing.

They would allow the Bible teacher to continue teaching, but just before her class period started, they had another teacher give an hour of intensive communist propaganda and indoctrination. During that class period, the students were taught several theories contrary to Christianity. They were educated on the theories of evolution and atheism, constantly being told that Jesus was only a regular man and that the Bible is a book of lies written by men who had been inspired by fantasy.

This indoctrination produced a generation of cynical children. They did nothing but mock and laugh at their Bible teacher once the second hour began. They ridiculed the stories she taught, oftentimes bringing her to tears. There was no discipline in these classes. The teacher had absolutely no control whatsoever.

Thankfully, the Word of God and the belief in His existence had been so consistently planted in my sisters' and my hearts that we were able to recognize the deception in the government's approach. Of course, we showed respect to both teachers, but no one was able to permanently break that foundation of faith that had been so strongly built in our early years.

It's just like the Bible says. If you direct a child along the right path, when he is old, he won't leave it.[1] **If you'll instill the right beliefs in your children today, the convictions will lie deep inside of them, springing up when they need them most.**

In Their Words

Rein's life is a tribute to how God can take our broken lives and craft them into something beautiful. To see his walk with the Lord and how he relates to God each and every day is humbling. He rarely even talks about the Lord without his voice quivering and tears of gratitude filling his eyes. His heart for the lost and his desire to bring people to the saving knowledge of Christ is evident in all he has done for the Kingdom of God on this earth. (Jana Lackey, Love Botswana)

---

[1] Proverbs 22:6

Live with Grit

During wartime, determination wasn't just encouraged; it was necessary for survival. Whether I was doing my homework or trying to procure food for my family, I always worked hard, as did my sisters. We didn't really know any different, since we grew up with my parents and grandparents who were four of the hardest working people I've ever known.

Most people worked at least half days on Saturdays back then, and every day was a full, nine- or ten-hour day. The forty-hour workweek is really just a recent invention. Back then, it was closer to fifty-two. I remember well Dad waking up before daylight, doing any necessary housework, and then leaving for work. He usually did not come home until after dark because he traveled either by public transportation or by bicycle. He was typically gone from seven o'clock in the morning to seven o'clock at night.

When Dad was growing up, men were encouraged to learn a trade first and then to attend school on the weekends once they started working. This helped out those who couldn't afford a university, those whose family had no status, and those who wanted to work as an electrician, engineer, etc. This was the route Dad chose. He trained as a tool and dye maker, and then he later went to school to become an engineer.

These weren't Dad's only talents. By hobby, he was a poet and an artist. It seemed that just about any birthday or holiday, he was presenting a new poem. I think the arts were the channel through which he best expressed his thoughts and feelings. He played the trumpet in the church band, and we often held the practices in our home. Both he and Mother also sang in the church choir.

At Christmastime, he would teach songs or poems to us children and have us recite them at parties and in church services. People always seemed to look forward to hearing them. Sometimes, he even traveled and preached in churches throughout Berlin. Later, during tough economical times, he used his artistic skills to make extra money for the family.

We were always thankful for Dad's drawing, designing, technical and scientific abilities because they kept him from having to go into the army. His job was so needed at the time that he was selected to work in a design office under contract by the German defense department. He worked as a constructional designer and later as a technical engineer.

He helped design the equipment used to manufacture Hitler's "secret weapons," which included the V-1 flying bomb and the V-2 rocket. Although Dad was naturally extremely talented, he never took that talent for granted. He understood that success was a result of much more than natural ability; it was a result of focus, grit, and sheer determination.

Sometimes, Dad had to work harder than most because of the values he chose to live with. Unlike most of his friends, the government hadn't deceived him. He was not going to give into beliefs he felt were wrong. Dad recognized the immorality and indecency that was being encouraged by the Third Reich under the leadership of Hitler, whom Oma called the Iron Broom because of his terrible eventual "sweeping" of the Jews back to Palestine, which she believed fulfilled prophecy in Scripture. So he made up his mind that he would never join the Nazi Party. Many people who were against the Nazis did what they "had" to do. They joined the Nazi party, just to "get ahead." But Dad never did.

After the war, because he wouldn't reform to the ideology of communism and join the Communist party, Dad got demoted and transferred to another office on the outside of Berlin. Everyone seemed to be surprised by this demotion because of his talent level, experience, and the length of time he had been with the company. Of course, Dad was frustrated, but he still honored his employers.

He treated them with respect and never talked badly of them to us. That made a great impression on me, as I'm sure it did on everyone watching him. Dad made it known that, even if you're slighted, you must keep working hard, working well, and working with a good attitude. He truly lived out the Bible verse instructing us to work willingly at whatever we do, as though we are working for the Lord rather than people[2].

This work ethic is one piece of my inheritance that has made all the difference in helping me become who I am today. I wouldn't be who I am as a follower of Christ, husband, father, businessman, or philanthropist without the understanding that life takes grit. As David

---

[2] Colossians 3:23

Brinkley says, **"A successful man is one who can lay a firm foundation with the bricks others have thrown at him."** Sometimes, you've just got to keep working.

Don't Let Small Stop You

At eighteen years old, I emigrated from Germany to Canada to escape the communism of East Berlin and to begin pursuing a career. Even then, I never forgot the valuable lessons that my parents instilled in me. Sure, the thought crossed my mind several times: I was away from my parents and was free to do whatever I wanted! But I had seen what had worked for them. I knew that I didn't want to stray from their moral ideas.

Of course, I was not perfect or nearly close to it, but I never got into any major trouble. I see now that it was the instruction of my parents, the prayers of my grandparents, and the inherited desire to succeed that helped to keep my life on the right path.

That's why today, I strive to never take my role as a parent lightly. No matter how small of an impact we as parents might think we're making, our influence is infinitely more important to our children's future than we could ever imagine. Even when our words of wisdom seem like they're falling on deaf ears, they aren't. What's sowed today often isn't reaped until much later. The moments we create for them now can truly shape their future.

This idea doesn't just pertain to parenting. Whatever we do, as a spouse, as a friend, or as someone chasing a dream, we can be confident that **sowing today will produce a harvest tomorrow. It doesn't matter where we come from, how many bad experiences we have had, or how little we start with.** All that matters is that we start, making the most of what we have been given. All that matters is that we recognize the defining moments in our own lives and respond to them well.

No one would have thought that a young man growing up in poverty during World War II could have later led a business like Chemcraft, the one that I was privileged to lead. No one would've thought that a man who later entered two broken relationships could one day build a God-honoring and fulfilling marriage. But because of parents who taught me about the value of family, the presence of God, and the importance of hard work, I did just that.

As long as we value the right parts of life and never let our circumstances keep us from pursuing greatness, we *can* achieve our goals. We can discover the reason we were placed on this earth and pursue that purpose to its full potential.

Throughout the years, I learned the importance of taking advantage of every moment—of building the moments you can and responding well to the ones that are built for you. Because soon enough, you'll wake up to find that those moments have added up to create a life—*your* life.

2

How to Have Peace in Chaos

A Country in Conflict

I hear the sounds of the people more loudly now. The adults are talking, and the young children are playing outside of the center. I'm saddened by their conditions, but it seems that they are already learning the lessons I was forced to learn during the terrible bombings and unwanted evacuations. They're realizing that no matter what's going on around them, they can be content.

We all can. We can be filled with God's peace on the inside, because we know that the level of joy we live with does not depend on our circumstances. The sooner we all realize this, the more satisfying our lives will be, no matter who or what is causing instability around us. In the midst of chaos, we can always find peace.

My first encounter with Hitler was at seven years old while at a special parade held in downtown Berlin. With all the commotion going on, I felt like we were at Disneyland. I was enjoying myself, but it was obvious that my parents were on edge. I wanted to know why. As the tanks rolled in, it became apparent that the

Wehrmacht, the German Armed Forces, was in charge of this event and that *Der Führer,* the leader himself, was present. The parade was enormous and brimming with nervous excitement.

The march began in front of the Brandenburg Gate, a famous spot in Berlin, often recognized as the location Pres. John F. Kennedy gave his "Ich bin ein Berliner" speech in 1963. Other famous speeches were given here, including the one in which Pres. Ronald Reagan so passionately exclaimed about the Berlin Wall, "Mr. Gorbachev, tear down this wall!"

You could feel it in the air: this too was about to become a part of history.

The scene was more than my little senses could take in. The streets were packed and smelled of sweat and smoke. Hundreds of thousands of people stood like a mindless herd of cattle, watching as columns upon columns of soldiers marched in step and special vehicles pulled the artillery. The army's emotions were hard, and their faces were set like stone. Their motions were robotic but ardent, nonetheless.

I sat high on Dad's shoulders, watching in awe, as one by one, soldiers carrying torches raised them in the air, yelling "Sieg heil" ("Hail victory") to Hitler as he passed by. I was amazed at how one man drew so much attention.

It was hard to focus on one thing. I wanted to watch Hitler but couldn't keep my eyes off the people around me. They were passionate. They seemed caught up in the moment, like they felt they were becoming a part of something bigger than themselves. They were impressed with Hitler, and their pride showed all over their faces. Surely, they didn't all know this man. But they felt something for him. Was it respect? Or was it fear? I couldn't tell.

It was obvious Mother and Dad thought differently of Hitler than most of those at the parade did. They didn't yell; they just watched quietly, until finally Dad muttered, "This is trouble. Where is it all going to end?"

The setting was more than eerie. We all knew it. We all felt it. My little seven-year-old self was unsure of why but was glad when Dad decided it was time to head home.

My sister Ursula and I were the only ones born by this time. We were still young, so my parents shielded us from the worst of the news. We didn't really know much about Hitler. The bit of information we did know was that several years before, on January 30, 1933, the German people elected him as their leader.

At that time, because of indecision in the government, Germany had been facing budget problems. Hitler saw that as his opportunity to make grand promises—promises that he never intended to keep. The German people believed in his promises, which ultimately turned out to be nothing more than a series of sly tricks. They fell for many of Hitler's grand guarantees, but their biggest hope was placed in his promise to abolish the administration they had come to resent. However, instead of protecting our country, his leadership is what ultimately destroyed it.

The destruction wasn't sudden. Hitler played his cards well. He was smooth, inching his way into the hearts of Germans until he convinced the majority of them that his way was the right way, the only way. We weren't in that majority. We obeyed the Nazis but never out of a desire to please them. We obeyed them out of fear for safety.

As the war progressed, the propaganda minister, Dr. Joseph Goebbels, promised almost daily that there was progress on all fronts and that Germany would soon gain complete victory. He was what they called a silver mouth, comparable to our news media today. Because Goebbels was closer to Hitler than anyone, people believed him, until little by little, horrible event after horrible event, we discovered that the information he gave was meant to keep us calm rather than to give us the truth.

One of his poorest decisions at the start of the war was purposely misinforming us that bombs would never fall on Germany. Because they fell all right. And they didn't stop, until many had lost their lives or the lives of those they loved.

In It Together

After months of fleeing to our homemade bunkers during air raids, Hitler ordered community bunkers to be built throughout the entire city. They were much stronger than our homemade effort, constructed with a five-foot-thick roof and three-foot-thick walls of steel and concrete. It always felt, looked, and smelled dirty and wet inside. Each bunker held a few hundred people, with every family assigned to its own little cabin. The cabins were small, with a couple of bunk beds, four or five high.

There were at least three stacks of bunks in each room. The kids slept on top, and the adults slept on the bottom. Night after night, I lay in that bed, staring up at the ceiling, wondering what my future held. Night after night, I struggled to convince myself that I would see the sun rise again. But morning after morning, I did, and I thanked God for it.

The bunker we used was half a block from our house, on the same side of the street. A group of Italian men were hired to build it, and one of them lived with us while they did. As a young boy, I loved watching and learning about all the different machines. They even let me climb on the enormous steam shovels and ride with them. I was disappointed when they left, but we kept in touch. They often sent over cheap wine from Italy, and we thought it was the greatest gift. Even the cheapest of wines was a luxury for us back then.

Our family was fortunate that the bunker was close to home because we only had a few minutes to get there before the enormous iron doors closed. Many nights, we ran in a panic, barely making it before the doors shut tightly. I often compared those huge doors to Heaven's gates. Watching people get left out in the warzone made me certain I wanted to know more about Salvation, more about how to make it through the eternal gates and into Heaven when this life was over.

During this time, black outs were also required all throughout the city. Curtains had to be down or windows had to be painted so that the light would not be shining from your house. The government believed that if the bombers saw light, they would know where to bomb. Every day, they sent noncommissioned police officers to closely monitor these blackouts. If you had light shining out for any period of time, they would find you quickly and order you to cover it up.

I grew to dread nighttime. The raids were infrequent in the beginning, but they occurred more frequently as time progressed, and they were frightening beyond belief. At the worst of the war, bombs fell two to three times a week. To prepare, every evening after dinner and before bed, we laid out our clothes because once the sirens went off, we only had ten minutes to dress and get to the bunker. It was especially hard the times a bomber would hit a power plant or transformer, and the whole area would lose what little electricity we had. It was not easy scrambling around in the dark!

Fear and trepidation lit the faces of every person stumbling into the shelter, awakened from their sleep only moments before by the earsplitting sound of the sirens. I paid attention to the other families running alongside us. Most only consisted of mothers and children, since the fathers were gone, serving somewhere on the German frontlines.

Despite the negative thoughts and emotions that wanted to overtake me, I knew deep down that I should be grateful. I had more than most. I had my father, while most of my friends' fathers had been drafted. Thankfully, forty years was the cutoff age, and Dad had turned forty-one just months before the war began.

Things felt so much safer with him home to lead and protect us.

I may not have known much about God at seven years old, but there is one thing I knew beyond a shadow of a doubt: He was real, and He was watching out for us. He had to be. Time and time again, we survived raids, drafts, evacuations, and illnesses. No one could convince me that those were coincidences.

One raid usually lasted about twenty minutes. It was twenty minutes of sheer terror while we prayed desperately for our lives and the lives of those we loved to be spared. As we waited in the cold, wet cell-like room, our biggest fear was that a percussion bomb would hit the bunker directly and crack it open. If it did, we were all dead. The bombs would eat up the oxygen, and everyone inside would suffocate. The British used napalm bombs then, which were incredibly effective. Nothing living could escape from them.

The all-clear siren incited feelings of both relief and dread. Relief because we had survived another bombing, but dread as many felt their hearts couldn't handle seeing one more friend or family member gone or their entire life's work shattered and destroyed.

Nevertheless, when the great iron door opened, everyone hurried out, emerging from the bunker, wondering what they would find. Each time it was like opening a surprise package, only one you weren't looking forward to opening. Most of the time, we found parts of our beloved city destroyed, sometimes with thousands of people dead. Thankfully, we lived on the fringes of the city, and the worst attacks were made toward the center. Still, it was terrible.

Both the sight and smell were unlike anything you could imagine. Hearing the uncontrollable sobs of those recognizing the ash-covered face of a loved one sent chills up your spine. The smell of burning bodies and buildings quickly became etched in my mind as the smell of death. Every day, death became more and more real. It brought the unwelcomed reminder that our lives could be taken at any moment.

Although Mother wouldn't let us near the rubbish, I knew the soldiers and volunteers were recovering bodies from the debris. My heart ached for those families who had to bear watching the bodies of their loved ones be collected, with no proper burial, no proper homage paid to their life. It was as if each person was just another German body "to get out of the way," as Hitler might say.

We typically had a few hours at home before the next siren sounded. Some families gave up on going back at all and started spending their nights in the shelters. Many gave up on changing clothes and sometimes on going to sleep at all. Ursula sometimes cried from nightmares and didn't want to sleep. On the contrary, I always tried to go to sleep because even if I did have nightmares, they were better than the reality I was living in.

Every time I think back on this time of my life, the sirens remind me of an invaluable truth: that I am to heed the warnings given to me, whether through Scripture, people I trust, or past experiences so that

I will not put myself in harm's way. **God often puts these bits of wisdom in our path for a reason, and if we pay attention to them, they can save us from destruction.**

Through every bombing, we were extremely fortunate in getting to the bunker on time, surviving the raid, and still having our home when we returned. But one night, we had a close call. We came out to a huge hole in our house, with half the roof tiles gone and most of the windows shattered. For months, Dad and Opa worked hard to restore and repatch things.

Although we were upset about the damage, we were relieved that no one was hurt. Because it was such a rush to get to the bunker, my grandparents generally chose to stay in the house, just as they had that night. It was as much of a risk physically for them to rush to the bunker than it was to take their chances in the house.

Each bombing after the first intensified, causing Berlin to become an increasingly dangerous place to live in. It wasn't long before the women of the Nazi party spoke up, insisting that the women and children of Berlin be evacuated. They anticipated more bombing raids and knew that they wouldn't have enough room in the hospitals to look after everyone. The German government agreed and decided to move the families eastward behind the German troops.

By that time, the troops had gone into Poland and were moving in toward Stalingrad (now Volgograd), Russia. So they took people to East Prussia. Families were picked according to a random system, but they tried to rid of big families first.

We were a fairly large family, so one day toward the beginning of the selection process, we got picked. We weren't forced to go, but we were strongly encouraged to for our protection, so we did. That was the first time I had ever heard the term *evacuation*, but it sure wasn't going to be my last.

Evacuation to Prussia

I remember well Mother packing up our little suitcases one foggy morning in the spring of 1942, after the air raids became more threatening. Dad was not allowed to go with us. They needed him to stay back and work with his team on a special project for the war effort. Early one morning, he took Mom, Ursula, and me to a special railway station. There were rows of long train cars set up, all with doors open, as if they were inviting us into safety. I was just a young boy, so the excitement of riding a train and then later a ship outweighed most of the feelings of fear.

However, once I saw the train, I had my questions. At the front, there were a couple of cars with sandbags, just in case the partisans decided to try and blow us up. I remember looking at those carts, encouraging myself. I was scared and felt a lot like that train traveling through a dark tunnel, with no end in sight.

When would this darkness be over? Would I ever see light again? But I knew that I had Someone who was going before me, just like those padded carts. I had my Father God, who was more than able and more than willing to keep me safe and free from harm.

Every time I thought about what could happen, I would remind myself that I had Someone driving my train who knew the end from the beginning and that Someone would take care of me. These thoughts kept me at peace in the midst of chaos.

After a lengthy wait, the station called, and out we went. Men and women in uniforms ran around blowing whistles and shouting at people to get on the train. Hesitantly, we boarded. A worker lifted me up and put me into a compartment, right next to my mother and sister. I looked around. The station was a madhouse.

Workers ran around frantically, checking people off their lists. They sternly informed us that we would get off at a certain stop, and at that stop, someone would be there to pick us up. The train filled quickly. Now it was time to say good-bye. Mother's arms reached out to hold Dad's one more time, with tears streaming down her cheeks. He tried to comfort her as he fought through his own.

This was the first time since they had been married that Mother and Dad had to be apart for any considerable length of time. What's worse is that with the severity of the war, there was a great chance that this good-bye could be their last. They tried to hide the seriousness of it all from us, but I knew, and I desperately hated it.

How could these people be so heartless? Could they not see that they were ripping families apart? Or did it simply not bother them, as they sat in their cozy homes with their happy families, feasting on foods that we could only dream of gracing our dinner table? My mind was going wild at that thought as people moved frantically around me. The train lurched forward, and as it did, my mind settled. There was nothing I could do now. We were leaving behind all we knew.

From then on, everything was unknown: our home, our safety, and our health. We didn't know what would happen the next hour, much less the next day, week, or year. We had to learn to take life one day at a time, thanking God for each one and living each as if it was our last.

After hours of traveling, it grew dark, just as we were rolling into our stop in a small remote part of East Prussia. We got out, and one of the representatives from the women's organization called for "the Preik family."

We hesitantly lifted our little hands along with Mother's and were swiftly introduced to a man in a horse and buggy. His name was Herr Krauser. He was a quiet large man, with not much to say to us. We piled into his horse-drawn buggy, and about a half hour later, we arrived at his small farm.

The Krausers took us in for the next several months. They were sweet people, although I'm sure they felt inconvenienced, since the government forced them to take us in. They were not wealthy by any means, and because of the layout of their home, there was absolutely no privacy for either family. We had to walk through each other's rooms to get in and out of the house.

The American idea of farms is much different than what Prussian farms were like back then. Prussian farms were relatively small and not well kept, since most of them were self-sustaining. The Krausers had pigs, cows, horses, chickens, and geese. Animals were milked and slaughtered when food was needed. There was really no way to keep the farm clean or warm in the midst of freezing temperatures.

When we pulled up to the Krausers' farm, it was dark. Herr Krauser walked us up the stairs and into a small room under the gable roof lit by a couple of petrol lamps. It was right by the smoke room, which was a part of the chimney and had just one bed. As soon as Mother saw it, she started crying. After the Krausers left, I heard her whisper to herself, "How are we all going to live here, in this little room? It's impossible."

There was just one bed for all three of us, but we were all so tired it didn't seem to matter much to us that first night. We laid the few pieces of luggage that we had in the corner and collapsed onto the hard mattress. In the morning, we woke up to a full view of the humble farmhouse. It consisted of two bedrooms, a sitting room, and a kitchen. Mom had to use the farmer's kitchen, which was upsetting for a woman who loved cooking as much as she did.

Cleanliness was a big deal to Mother. At home, she made us wash our hands and feet and go to bed clean every night. But that wasn't how the farmers lived. They would go into the barn to milk a cow and then come right back into the house. If they stepped into dirt or manure, they didn't even wash their feet!

Mother got so undone over their way of living that she would physically shake just like she did in the bunker, and we would have to calm her down. It didn't really bother me, though! I was just excited to see the pigs and cows up close. There were a lot of new things for me to focus on to distract me from what I had lost.

It was a different lifestyle for sure, but we had no choice but to cope with it and to remind ourselves that we were blessed simply to be alive. As the days passed, I came to the stark realization that there was no stopping life. No matter what was going on, women would still be having babies, and men would still be going off to war. I couldn't just stop everything to try to cope with what was going on. Life was moving right along, and in the midst of all the craziness, it was up to me to learn to deal with it.

Making the Most of It

Life during wartime left little room for control. It felt as if you were on a train bound for disaster. You had no choice but to be on the train and no choice but to stay on it. You could walk from cart to cart, in any direction you wanted, but no matter what, the train was still headed for trouble. You just had to try and be as comfortable as you could along the way.

Our parents understood where this war-train was headed, but we didn't. We heard the whispers and could pick out the fear and doubt in our parents' voices, but we didn't fully understand what was going on. We just knew our lives weren't normal. Children in *normal* conditions played with their toys and imaginary friends. They didn't live in bunkers and search for spent antiaircraft shells for fun.

There's no question that war caused us to grow up more quickly than most kids. Still, we always had fun and made the most of our circumstances. Sometimes this meant befriending an animal we pretended was a pet. Sometimes it meant sneaking down to the watermill to play. Whatever it was, we did our best to forget the train's destination and focus on having fun along the way. That was really all we could do!

Despite the trouble we had with the farm, there was a beautiful simplicity about living there. The farmers pretty much did everything themselves, which often presented us kids with opportunities for fun.

When Herr Krauser brought in the hay from the field, he would call Ursula and me to ride in his horse-drawn wooden cart, on top of the haystack. We would be at least eight feet high. We loved riding like we were a king and queen being paraded into our kingdom, waving and bowing to our make-believe parishioners. Mother stood by nervously laughing, ready at any moment to jump out and catch us if we were to fall. We weren't nervous though. We were having fun!

Herr Krauser often let me go on little excursions with him. Some of my favorites were riding on his horse and buggy and visiting the old-fashioned flourmill. At the mill, there was no mechanization; everything was done by hand. I loved watching as the water rode overtop of the water wheel, which in turn powered the flourmill. When grain was put in, flour came out, and it was sifted and grinded again and again until it was fine enough to be used.

What was work to the farmers was fun to a little eight-year-old boy with nothing else to do! Sometimes I would even wake up early to watch them milk the cows and get the milk ready to sell. Watching them kill a pig or a chicken was a little scarier, but I still couldn't keep away!

"Watch, boy!" Herr Krauser would yell as he cut the head of the chicken off. The body ran around like it was trying to find its misplaced head. After I got over the shock, I burst into laughter. What a sight!

One of our favorite places to play (and maybe cause a little mischief!) was in Herr Krauser's barn. We often sneaked off when Mother wasn't watching and climbed up the ladder and into the rafters, squealing with delight as we planned our jumps. A belly flop, a flip, a backward drop—we loved the feeling of free falling into the hay bales.

The only problem with our setup was the fact that each section was separated by about a foot in length. One day, I watched little Ursula jump and squeal with delight as she prepared to hit the hay. But that squeal of delight soon turned into a cry of panic when she realized that she was headed right for one of those foot-long gaps. She disappeared, and my heart sunk. How was I going to get her out? At that time, I was just a little guy myself!

I tried to come up with every possible solution that would keep me from having to tell the farmer about our secret, but I finally decided that I couldn't get her out on my own. I reluctantly told him about our little game gone wrong. After a quick scolding, I stood on the side, scared, waiting for him to pull Ursula out. Thankfully, besides a few scratches, she was fine. After a few hours, the fear wore off, and we were back into our mischief-making ways, finding another way to have a little fun.

That was an easy task, considering that the area of Prussia that we stayed in was in the countryside, right across from Lithuania, which Germany had recently occupied. We lived right by a lake that seemed pretty big to an eight-year-old. There was a fishery about a quarter mile away, so I used to take off and visit it often. I got to know the owner, Mr. Liebe, well. It was really the only social interaction I had, besides the little bit I had with fellow students in the schoolhouse. We were extremely isolated on the farm.

I spent a lot of time there with Mr. Liebe. It became the highlight of my time in Prussia. Sometimes, he would allow me to go out with the crew to fish, as their bait boy. My job was to drag the nets to catch the bait in the shallows. I didn't swim then, so I kept the details from Mom to prevent her from worrying.

One day, I decided to take Mr. Liebe's little rowboat out by myself. I felt pretty independent. Unfortunately, as soon as I got out, I realized that the boat wasn't solid. The bottom fell out, and the boat sank. Immediately, a wave of panic and fear rushed over me. I couldn't swim! I fished around for any parts of the boat that I could grab onto. I held on tightly and paddled my way back to shore.

When I got home, I was soaked and shaken up. I can't remember what I told my mother, but I could see that she had been worried. I was fine though, and she was happy when she saw that I had brought fish home.

Another time, four boys who were older than I was asked me to go on a little sailing excursion with them. I was so excited to be invited that I didn't even think about safety. We left early one afternoon, intending to get home before it got dark that night. But once we had gotten to the other side of the lake and into Lithuania, a vicious storm hit. We didn't know what to do. One of the boys suggested that we try our best to get to the shore, which was directly across from our homes, and then walk back around the lake. It was a far walk, but we all agreed.

We struggled with the sails until we landed onshore, and then we began the long trek home. We were a little afraid to travel by foot for a couple of reasons. First of all, it was beginning to grow dark, and the area was unfamiliar to us. Second, we thought we might encounter German army patrols or partisans. We knew we probably weren't supposed to be there and didn't want to get into any trouble.

Still, we walked, and I struggled to keep up in the dark. We walked all night, soaking wet and freezing. The sun was just peering above the horizon as we approached home. When we arrived, we learned that our families had called the local police unit, and they had sent motorboats out to search for us. Once I saw Mother's worried face, I felt bad, but I sure had fun telling my stories of survival! I made up for it, again, by bringing fish home.

Some foods, like fish, were a delicacy to us then. If we didn't want the fish, we would trade them with the farmers for other treats. Normally, Mom took pride in being able to prepare great meals, but our living arrangements made that hard for her. There were no stores close by for her to buy us food from. On top of that, we didn't have much money—just the little bit that Dad sent us when he could. When we had some money, Mother had to beg for a ride to the store with the farmer on his horse and buggy.

It's in times like these that you truly learn to be thankful for what you do have rather than directing your attention toward what you don't have. **If your focus is right, then even in the midst of a frustrating time, you can be content.** No matter where you are or what circumstances you're up against, you can always find a reason for joy because **joy is not based on your outer circumstances; it's based on the condition of your heart.**

In Their Words

Rein has an amazing sense of humor. Even in stressful times, he does things to make it fun. We often rode on planes together and liked to talk business. After a while, he would want to change the mood to keep things light. He knew I was always misplacing stuff, so if I got up to go to the washroom or to grab a drink, he would take my calendar or one of my

> *books and hide them. I'd come back, and he'd see me searching frantically for it. He was so good at hiding that he took it! It got to the point that if I lost something, I'd go straight to him and ask, "Did you take it?" Of course, he'd always deny it, but somehow he always knew where to find it! I was always grateful for that sense of humor. It really has never left him. (David Rogers, CEO, Chemcraft International)*

Peace in Chaos

The more I learned to set my heart on the good, the calmer each day seemed. But there was still one place I had an extremely hard time focusing: school.

The school we attended in Prussia was a one-room schoolhouse a little less than a two-mile walk away. Before that time, I'd never heard of a one-room schoolhouse. There were about twenty-five students altogether, with five or six of them evacuating from Berlin. It was confusing to me at first because there were five-year-olds and fifteen-year-olds in the same class, and everyone was being taught different things!

They placed the younger ones at the front, and then they made their way back to the older ones. Later on, they separated us with the younger ones on the left side and the older on the right side. Either way, it was just as confusing!

In Berlin, I always made good grades, but when I got into that classroom, I had problems keeping up because I got so distracted. I was in grade 3 but thought what they were learning in grade 4 and grade 5 sounded much more interesting! The teacher was talking about "algebra," a term I hadn't yet heard but wanted to learn about much more than the simple addition and subtraction on my section of the chalkboard. I wanted to keep up with the older kids. I'll never forget bringing home my report card that semester. My mother was shocked at my low scores.

The kids were rowdier in Prussia than in Berlin. I was bored and had no interest at all, so I often got caught up in their antics. (There was one thing that struck my interest while I was there though. It was the first time I thought a girl was cute. I even followed her home one day to find out where she lived!) Nevertheless, I continued to try harder to pull my grades up, but it took major effort to keep my attention on the right thing.

Learning to fix my focus in school helped me fix it in other parts of my life. I found that to live in peace, I simply could not give attention to my outer circumstances. They were too unstable. Instead, I had to keep my heart set on hope, trusting that everything would work out to its proper end. It's the same for all of us. **Living a life of peace requires us to be content on the inside, believing that everything is under control even when it doesn't seem that way. In times of chaos and conflict, we don't have to be shaken.**

With Ursula and a friend on our first day of school, 1939

On the Road Again

Keeping my focus right got me through this time in Prussia. Thankfully though, it was only a few months before Dad showed up to take us elsewhere. My Opa had a brother living near Konigsberg at the time, so Dad took us there. We were relieved to be with family, but that stay didn't last long either.

We were there for about a week when we heard that the German offensive was facing problems in Stalingrad and was going to have to retreat. The German fighter planes and artillery began to frequent our skies, and we soon realized the war was headed our way. There was too much commotion for us, Dad said, and so he decided that we would move back to Berlin. During our time at home, Sigi was born, which added some joy to those stressful days.

We were only in Berlin for a few months before Dad's design group was ordered to transfer to Sudetenland (which was a part of Germany then but later became Czechoslovakia) into a town called Haida. Because Dad's work was confidential, his life was constantly at risk there, but he never let Mother or us kids know the extent of it. He never even took us to the place where he worked. Everything about his job had to be kept top secret.

When leaving Berlin for Haida, we were informed that we could take some furniture and clothing with us, as well as any other items we wanted to take, as long as they could fit into a small part of the railway car assigned to us. We filled it with as much as we could, and it was shipped to Haida for us to pick up when we arrived.

Opa and Oma had to stay behind, for two reasons. First of all, they didn't get permission to move; and second, it was just as taxing on their frail bodies to move than to stay and endure the bombings. During wartime, the Germans who went to war left many jobs open and unfilled. This became a problem for the

German economy. To fix it, the German government forced Polish workers to move to Germany and take their place.

In order to house them, they required any Germans with extra space in their homes to open them up to the Polish. Because we had left for Haida, the government forced Oma and Opa to take a few of the workers in. This was especially hard on them, since they were older. They did not know these people, and there was no established trust between them. It was also extremely difficult to communicate since they did not speak the same language.

Mother and Dad left for Haida first so that they could look for a place to live. They took Ursula with them, and then they came back for Sigi and me later. Right after they left, they heard on the radio that Berlin had just experienced its heaviest bombing raid yet.

They made it back to us as quickly as possible, surviving a major train strafing along the way. On their way home, the whistle blew several times as the train stopped, and they had to hurry off and into the bushes, as their train car was repeatedly shot at. When they told me about their experience, I was shaken up. I imagined little Ursula screaming, crying, and holding tightly to Dad's hand as the plane swooped down, machine guns rapidly firing at them.

Everything in me wished I had been there with my family. I almost felt guilty for being safe at home, absent from the terror that their hearts must have felt. Some people were killed, but thankfully, they made it to us, and we all made it back to Haida together and in one piece. We were ready to start over, yet again.

Our family ended up residing in a rented pub meeting room. It was just one large room for all of us, but it worked out nicely. The area we lived in was hilly, surrounded by a forest, and the pub we were staying in was at the top of one of these hills. There was a dairy retail store down the hill from us, and in the wintertime, they often had trouble getting the milk delivered because the truck couldn't make it back up the hill in heavy snow.

When that happened, I would load up the back of a sleigh with two or three milk cans, jump on, and ride down, steering with my feet the whole way. Then I'd walk back up the hill and load up the next batch. Two trips a day were all I could really take before the snow melted. I might've spilled a little milk along the way, but somehow, I never crashed! I made myself a few marks helping them out and had loads of fun. (Plus, they gave me free milk!)

We were on food stamps in Haida, just like everyone else. To supplement the food stamps, Dad and I rented bikes and rode into the countryside to buy food directly from the farmers. It was cheaper that way, and it was the only way to get extra food.

Because of rationing, no one was allowed to buy anything extra in the stores, no matter how much money they had. We would be exhausted by the end of the day, but it was worth it. We usually covered about ten to fifteen miles, with three to four stops along the way. Dad took along some of his paintings, and we traded them with the farmers for food.

Sometimes, we got so hungry along our route that we had to ask a farmer for something to eat. Dad hated begging for himself, so he'd use me as the bait.

"My little boy here is starving," he'd say. "Do you have something for him to eat?"

Usually they gave me a piece of bread with butter. It's funny, but I can still taste it. The fresh rye bread and thick butter lathered on was like a feast to me at that time. Of course, I shared with Dad, but I could've eaten the whole thing myself!

During this time, our main focus was simply survival, but we always tried to find ways to add a glimmer of joy to each day. Sometimes that came in the simple form of a warm loaf of bread or a few pounds of potatoes we managed to find. On days like that, dinnertime became the highlight of the day.

We had a nice school to go to, but we were taken out quite often for something that they called youth corps. During the day, they took us out into a field to have us play war games, like capture the flag. We were in the middle of rocky hills, so it was rough. It seemed as though everything during that time was directed toward the war, toward teaching us how to fight.

Sometimes, they'd call out fathers and sons for target shooting practice in preparation for the military. They'd hand me a rifle, not quite of military status but certainly a real and fairly large rifle. I was a pretty good shot as a young boy. I used to have to hide my proud little smirk when I would beat Dad. I enjoyed that part!

We could never find a church that suited us there, although we attended a Lutheran church several times. We were Baptist, so we were not used to the formal manner in which Lutheran services were conducted. And since the Nazis were in control of the Lutheran Church at that time, it made it even less of a fit for us.

During this time that the Germans were in control, no Czech people wanted to admit that they were Czech. They wanted people to think they were German, so they spoke our language, which made things a little easier on us. My time in Haida was an eventful one, filled with memories I will not soon forget.

My sisters and I had a good time there. We learned to have fun with everything that didn't cost anything. We loved to ski, so we were ecstatic about living on a huge hill. On the side of the hill opposite from the dairy, we would ski down without restriction. We used old wooden skis with no ski boots or any of those fancy contraptions we use today. If you fell, you were sore for days! Despite the unplanned bombing raids, we still played outside, since the sirens gave us about five minutes warning to run to our place of safety.

The difference between the raids in Haida from those in Berlin was that in Haida, we could actually see the bombers coming. We could feel the constant vibrations. There were hundreds of planes, and if they got into trouble, which they did often, they dropped a lewd of bombs. There was no target area; they just dropped them whenever the plane was in trouble! So even away from Berlin, we were still involved in the war. Nowhere felt safe.

3
How Focus Determines Future

Finding What Matters

As I watch the kids playing out on the dirt roads, I think back to the roads my home rested on—the once beautiful, bustling streets of Berlin. After the war hit, the roads looked much different, much less welcoming, much more similar to the ones these precious people have lived on their whole lives.

It's here that these young people are learning one of the most important lessons any of us can learn: They're learning how to fix their focus. They don't worry about the latest fashion trends or newest gadgets on the market; they focus on the invisible parts of life because that's all they've got. And one day, that's all you and I will have as well. It's often said that what we focus on is what we move toward. So we should strive to focus on the good, on the lasting, on the things that matter.

"We're moving . . . again."

My stomach dropped. I'd heard these words many times in the past, but this time, it stung worse than ever before. Not because I loved the place I was living in and not because I had made friends that I did not want to leave. It stung because it seemed impossible. I had just returned from a six-week stay in the hospital and was still recovering from a severe case of scarlet fever. I could hardly think, much less process the thought of relocating again. But just because I was sick didn't mean the Russians were taking the invasion any slower. They came in quickly to set up their camps as the German armies moved out. The Russians sought out spies and stray German soldiers, collecting from them any weapons they could get their hands on.

My sister Ursula had come down with scarlet fever first, after picking it up at school. She was admitted into the hospital and returned back home within only a few days, but I wasn't so lucky. I couldn't keep any food down. I had glandular fever, which caused all the glands in my body to triple in size. At one point, my temperature got so high that I became delirious. My body was trying hard to fight off sickness. As if the illness wasn't enough, the unstable location of the hospital and the scarcity of its supplies only heightened my parents' level of concern for my condition.

The nurses were afraid that I would get diphtheria, so they kept me in isolation. That was hard for an eleven-year-old boy! I wanted to be with my family, but I could only see them when they came to visit by getting pushed by wheelchair to my window and looking out to where they would stand in front of the hospital. The building was three stories high, and I was on the top story. Once things got a little bit better, they moved me to the regular hospital area, until I was well enough to return home.

The six weeks I spent lying in that quarantined Catholic hospital room was one of the loneliest and most disconcerting times of my life. To be so ill during wartime was a tough thing in itself, but to be ill during an invasion was even worse. Not long after I got sick, the Russians moved into Haida. Their plan was to get to Germany, but some came through our town first.

The German soldiers weren't leaving that easily, though. They fought. Giant artilleries were mounted onto railway cars, with heavy guns that could shoot a long way, usually about ten to twenty kilometers. When those guns fired, they'd shake a building like an explosion would. That's why we were all so worried about the hospital. It was located right next to the railway, about one-fifth of a kilometer away. You could hear the sound of artilleries in front of it. Many of the men, regardless of age, were given grenade launchers to try and stop the Russian tanks from entering. Even in a building typically associated with safety, I felt as threatened as if I was lying out in the middle of the street.

What was surprising to me about this particular invasion was that the Russians didn't seem like mean people at all. In fact, even while they were kicking us out of Sudetenland, they were nicer to us than the Czechs were! Still, the attack came at an extremely unfortunate time, especially for me.

The Germans tried hard to stand their ground, but eventually they gave in. Many men were lost, and it just didn't seem worth it to lose the rest. At this point in the war, hundreds of men ages eighteen to forty had been replaced with older men, sometimes sixty or seventy years old. The army had to be rebuilt. We were desperate to defend the Fatherland. Seeing men my Opa's age, holding a rifle or a rocket seems odd now; but during wartime, just about anything could have been considered normal.

It's amazing how quickly a transitional government was established throughout Czechoslovakia. They had their own army ready to go in just weeks! Dad and I worried about Mom with the Russian soldiers and were extremely protective of her. She would dress herself unattractively, as would the other women at the time, hoping to lessen the possibility of being noticed and possibly taken advantage of by the Russian soldiers.

One tough part of living in Haida during that time was that there was little to no communication. No telephones were available, and newspapers had to stop being produced because of the tight economic condition. I realized this one day when I went into a store to buy a pencil for school. I overheard a German soldier asking for an old newspaper to put in his boots so that it would soak up some of the water as they marched. The owner replied that newspapers were precious, since they had gone out of production. Because we had no publications to give us the truth about what was going on, rumors spread like wildfire. Everyone was scared for their safety and for the safety of their families.

Every day, our surroundings became increasingly unstable, so much so that all Germans were eventually ordered by the Czech government to evacuate the country and return back to Germany.

Still, in my mind, moving back was scarier than living through the terrors of the Russian invasion. The border was about eighty kilometers away, and we would have to travel by foot, which was made even more strenuous by the fact that the path was a mountainous one. Once Mother realized how gaunt and weak I had grown during my illness, she too became extremely wary of leaving.

"Walter." I overheard her crying to my dad. "Look at him. He's so thin! There's no way he can make it."

I knew I felt bad during that sickness, but I never knew how bad it truly was until I saw Mother's reaction. At first glance, she burst into tears. I thought to myself, *What's wrong with her? I'm here!* Then I looked in the mirror. I was shocked at what I saw. I had lost a lot of weight and was pale in the face.

Mother tried to hide the extent of her concern from me, but the worry on her face was obvious. For days, she seemed to be having a breakdown. Finally, Dad gave in to her alarm. He went to the authorities and asked for a six-week reprieve. They granted it, and we went to work, trying hard to strengthen my heart, lungs, and legs for the trip.

During that entire period of my life, I felt like I was in a dream. Everything moved so fast that I felt like I couldn't catch up. My mind couldn't process the reality of my situation, and thinking back, that was probably a good thing. Perhaps it all would have been a bit too shocking to take in at once. Even if I did understand the chaos going on around me, I most likely wouldn't have known how to deal with it.

Captured

I regained strength by spending time with Dad, going on walks, and helping him with various projects. One day, he decided to take me on mountain paths while he did some drawing. He grabbed his easel and some chalk, and we were on our way. I sat off to the side while he worked on the drawings of the mountainside, when all of a sudden, two Russian soldiers with fast-fire rifles walked up to us. They didn't speak much German, but they managed to get their point across. They wanted us to go with them.

My heart was pounding.

"Are we going to be all right?" I asked Dad.

"Yes, we will be fine," he assured me.

We walked for a while until we came to a farm that had obviously been completely taken over by Russians. I had no idea where we were, but I felt like we were extremely far from home. There, it's not like the suburbs. Walking two or three miles out of the city brings you way outside of town.

As we got to the farm, I couldn't help but notice huge Russian tanks, trucks, and soldiers everywhere. A big fire was going, with a kettle cooking their supper in the middle of the yard. The soldiers had a weird smell about them. They smelled like smoke mixed with sweat. One of the friendlier soldiers offered us some borscht, which is a kind of cabbage soup, and a meat pie. They were a rough bunch but fairly friendly. I think the fact that I was a child softened them a bit. We ate it gratefully and in silence, wondering why we had been brought there.

After a few minutes, the soldiers began coming up to Dad one by one and asking him to draw them. Apparently, they had seen how good Dad was with his art, and they wanted to have some fun. He was quick with charcoal sketches, so he did one after another, until a man who spoke broken German walked up and interrupted him.

"Who are you, and what are you doing?" he asked sternly.

Dad talked to him for a while, and I tried not to pay too much attention.

The next thing I heard him say was "Tell your son to go home."

Dad instructed me to return to Mother and tell her what had happened. I was terrified to go all that way by myself. How was I supposed to remember how to get there? I had never walked those roads before that day! Each turn, I questioned myself. Once I realized I was on the right track, the worry for my safety disappeared, and the reality of Dad's possible danger took over. I wondered what they would do to him.

As soon as I ran through the front door, I filled Mother in. She too was worried. She knew, as we all did, that once a week, the Czech would take revenge on the people they found suspicious. They'd line them up in front of the city hall and shoot them. This thought drove her crazy. She *had* to find out why they had captured Dad and what they were going to do with him.

Thankfully, there was a man living close by who had become good friends with Dad. He was also an artist, and his wife was Czech. They found out details for Mom. They discovered that the Russians had put Dad in the town jail, charging him for acting as a spy. They thought he had been drawing them for intelligence purposes. These friends went into the jail to vouch for Dad, and we waited patiently, praying that he would return home safely. Finally, after several days, he did.

We didn't go on too many walks after that incident, but we found other ways to fill our time. One day, Dad decided we'd build a cart. He made it out of wood because no other materials were available at the time. This homemade cart resembled ones the Greeks used to build, with wooden wheels, a wooden axle, and a metal band tied around it to keep it together. This is what we thought we would use to carry necessities from Haida back to Berlin.

The Trip

After six weeks of planning and preparing, we loaded that little cart with a fraction of our most loved belongings and arranged to head home. In it, Mother packed some of her best bedding, china, silver, a few changes of clothing, and several extra diapers for Sigi, who was a baby at that time. It was heartbreaking to watch her leave behind many of her wedding gifts, including her precious silk, hand-embroidered linens Dad brought back for her from South America, expensive china, and goose feather pillows.

Early one morning, we got up to begin our strenuous journey. Dad pulled our wagon, Mother pushed Sigi in a stroller, and Ursula and I walked alongside them as we traveled to our meeting place. Although I had initially dreaded this day, I had since grown a little more excited about it. But that all changed moments after we arrived at our starting point.

When we got there, there were already several hundred other refugees waiting. I looked around. The setting was intense, not at all what my naïve eleven-year-old mind imagined it would be. Czech soldiers sat on horses, holding whips, waiting for us to get situated. In a matter of minutes, I felt the excitement I had worked up over the last six weeks disappear. It was going to be a long eighty kilometers. I was no longer looking forward to traveling up and down hillsides with hundreds of people.

Despite my efforts to prepare, I didn't feel I was in good enough shape to be moving so quickly. Mother did not look strong enough to push Sigi all that way, and in the hot July weather, I was concerned that the two dresses and coat she had on would cause her to overheat. Dad seemed as though he would fall behind pulling the wagon. How would we ever keep up?

We felt discouraged, but no one seemed to care about our condition. After all, there were many like us, and the soldiers felt they were doing us a favor just by being there. We held a lot of resentment toward the Czech soldiers, especially after this incident. When you're mistreated, it's hard to separate the bad from the good. Surely, there were some good-hearted soldiers, but we were too bitter to see it at the time.

We prepared ourselves, both physically and mentally, and after a few minutes of instruction, we were off. The soldiers were adamant about us making it to the border as fast as possible. There were times I thought to myself, *What if they aren't leading us back to Germany? What if this is all one big trick to lead us somewhere else, like Siberia or a concentration camp?* My little heart was full of fear.

We moved as fast as we could, my little lungs struggling to keep up with my body. But there was one problem we hadn't considered well enough: the land was not flat country. It had hills, which made things even harder, on us and on the wagon. We hadn't thought about the friction wood causes when it's constantly rubbing against more wood. But pretty soon, it became obvious.

The wheels started smoking and caught fire. Dad called me over to attempt putting it out. I tried everything I could think of, but nothing worked. We were falling behind, so finally, Dad made a decision: we would have to leave the cart behind. With hesitancy and a tinge of hopelessness, we dropped it. It was hard to fathom that everything we owned was now gone, either back in Haida or lying in a ditch, useless.

In that moment, I sort of felt like that wagon. I felt as if my heart had become too broken and heavy to finish the journey. I wanted to crawl into the ditch with all our things and be left behind. I wanted to give up, but I knew that wasn't an option.

The sound of whips cracking and shots being fired did exactly what the soldiers meant for it to do—it kept us in fear, fear that pushed us on. The air was getting warmer. Throughout the group, people were falling. Some from fear of being shot at, some from being whipped, and some from exhaustion. Czech soldiers yelled and hit those behind us on their numb, tired bodies. My own body ached terribly. But still, I hurried. I couldn't give up. Not now. Not ever. I would use my pain as fuel to finish.

Those soldiers might have meant to hurt us by making us leave everything behind, but what was meant for harm actually turned out for the best. When they thought they were tearing me down, they were actually building me up, making me stronger, and teaching my heart a lesson worth learning.

We All Have to Leave Our Wagons

The fact is that we all have a race to run, a purpose to fulfill. It's the reason we're alive. But the more we live, the more baggage we accumulate. Little did I know that later I'd hold the baggage of heartache from failed relationships and the baggage of fearing poverty from growing up with so little. In order to live my life to its fullest, I had to learn to leave the baggage behind. It's just a fact of life: **at some point, we all have to leave our wagons.**

This concept was something I had learned in Sunday school as a child, but I had never seen it played out so clearly as I did this day. I remembered hearing the teacher read from the Scripture, *"Let us strip off every weight that slows us down . . . And let us run with endurance the race God has set before us . . . by keeping our eyes on Jesus, the champion who initiates and perfects our faith.[3]"* Now, I understood.

It's what you focus on that you move toward. That day, I determined I would try to keep my focus on tomorrow rather than staying stuck on yesterday. As it's often said, you can't drive forward looking in the rearview mirror! It was time to let go of the baggage, fix my eyes on the goal, and keep pressing on.

A Great Awakening

Thankfully, we made that rough journey successfully. When we got to Berlin, the city was in shambles. At least 90 percent of the river bridges had been blown up to keep the Russian tanks from crossing. I was worried about what our home was going to look like and how Oma and Opa were, if they were even still alive. I was relieved when we found them alive, although they were half-starved. The house was a mess, but Opa and Oma had managed to keep themselves fed by keeping a garden, since they were too ill to stand in the food lines. There were rows of potatoes and vegetables where the flowers once stood.

---

[3] Hebrews 12:1–2

Opa outside of our house in East Berlin, 1952

We had a lot of work to do to get things back to normal. While I tried hard to forget a lot of what happened while we were gone, the wagon memory stayed etched in my mind. I began to wonder, *Why was I in this life-race? What goal was I supposed to be moving toward?* I felt empty, like I was missing something. So I began to search. Not long after returning to Berlin, we reconnected to our little church. It was in one of the weekend meetings that I found my answer—a real relationship with Jesus Christ.

Don't get me wrong, as I said before, I had known about Jesus. I had all the head knowledge from Oma's Bible stories. I just hadn't let the information in my head transition to my heart. I knew He was watching out for me; I just didn't know *Him*. I desperately wanted to, though. I knew that He was my answer. He held my purpose, and He would show me how to find it.

So in the spring of 1949, at fifteen years old, I accepted Jesus into my life during a church service. There was just something that captivated my heart when the pastor talked about Him. It was the first time I had heard Him and His love described so personally. I knew I wanted the type of relationship with Jesus that this pastor had, so I asked him to help me get it.

At first, I was excited and served God with passion. But as the years passed, that wore off. My faith got beat out by the pressures of a practical mind, and I soon began planning out the next stages of my life without seeking my God or His advice. I disregarded that special relationship, making the choices that seemed logical to me.

Once we were back in Berlin, I was reenrolled in school. The building was partially bombed. Half of the roof was gone, and the glass was gone, so they moved us into what used to be a pub. They kept the front open to sell beer, but the government took over all the meeting rooms for classrooms. We probably had two or three classrooms for twelve different age groups, but that was okay with me. After all, I had survived that one-room Prussian schoolhouse!

The school I attended in Berlin from 1939 to 1950 after it was refurbished. Photo taken in 1998.

Because the school I had attended in Haida was so advanced, they moved me straight into grade 6. I went to school through grade 10, and then I entered another school that prepared me to become a paint chemist. I graduated from there two years later and then emigrated to Canada, on a quest to escape the Communist system and build a new life. It took five years to become a citizen of Canada, so after three and a half years of working odd jobs, I enlisted in the Canadian Armed Forces.

When I found out that they were recruiting in Winnipeg, Manitoba, I traveled there. I had experience working in a hospital at one of my odd jobs, so I applied for the medical corps. I got the job and entered medical training. There, we got basic education on first aid and battlefield injuries. In the corps, I also became a cross-country runner and was on the swim team.

In one of my classes one day, we were discussing limits. I asked my instructor about how long someone would be able to stay under the water. He told me that if someone stayed under too long, the person's body would eventually float up, so I thought I would try it.

Well, it didn't quite work out like my instructor had said. I tried, but the next thing I knew, I was lying by the poolside. I had stayed under too long, and my lungs couldn't handle it. I passed out in the water! Despite a few incidents like that, I had a wonderful time serving in the Canadian Army. There were certainly more hurdles for me than there were for most, but I enjoyed the challenge. Of all the physical and emotional barriers I could have faced, the biggest barrier seems quite silly compared to most—learning the English language.

On one of the IQ tests, I tested far below my level because I couldn't understand half of the questions! Later, I just so happened to come across some of the administrative papers, and I saw one that read, "Reinhold Preik – English, below standard."

I was disappointed in myself, but I had to remember that I was at a disadvantage. I hadn't had any education on the English language. Instead, I had to pick it up here and there. Over time, I finally started learning how to form words and sentences. It grew stronger the more I worked on it, but even now, I am still learning! To this day, I'm reluctant to use computers, which is a fear that probably stems from how uncomfortable I was with learning a new language.

> ### In Their Words
>
> *Dad is still getting used to the English language. Some of my best memories are of him waking us up by singing "Oh, What a Beautiful Morning" from Oklahoma in his thick German accent. I also loved hearing him completely mangle quotes. My favorite? Instead of "That's the way the cookie crumbles," he'd say, "That's the way the cracker breaks into little pieces." I could never hide my laugh! (Austin Preik, son)*

One of the reasons that I had initially joined the armed forces is because I had heard that it would give me a better chance of getting my citizenship granted early. And it did!

I was overjoyed when I could tell my service had made a difference. The judge asked, "So you're in the army, huh?"

"Yes, sir," I replied. "This country is going to grant me citizenship. I think I owe it to its people to serve them."

He liked that answer! I felt honored to finally have my Canadian citizenship.

Reconnected

One day, while training for the Canadian Army Medical Corps swim team, I had an accident. For whatever reason, that day I had decided to do a sailor's dive instead of a real dive, and I hit my head on the bottom of the pool. I was rushed to the hospital and received report of an injured skull. My teeth were filed down, and I was put on leave for about ten days in Barrie, a small city nearby. While on leave, a corporal I had known was attending a church called Immanuel Baptist. He decided to take me with him. I felt at home there, so I continued to go. As I did, I started to feel my faith in God come alive again.

My injuries were severe, so while I was healing, I couldn't do much but lie in bed in the barracks at the army camp. It was there that my mind began to wander. I began to think about my life and where it was headed. As I lay in bed, with that all-too-familiar feeling of emptiness, I remembered how my life had once been, back when God was in it fully. I realized that somewhere along the way, I had lost sight of what really mattered.

I'd switched my focus from my purpose to what *I* had wanted—money, positions, my citizenship. I let the baggage of my past—the fear of poverty and a sense of not belonging—weigh me down. Never once since my teenage years had I stopped to think about what *God* wanted for my life. I knew I needed Him back in control. I needed to remember the words of my childhood Sunday school teachers—ones that taught me that His plans are always good, and they're *always* greater than my own.[4]

---

[1] Jeremiah 29:11

It was right then that I decided: I was going to reconnect with God. I wanted that relationship again, and this time, for good. This time, I wouldn't forget. I wouldn't lose focus. So right there, on that cold concrete floor, I knelt at my bed; and with a shaky voice, I prayed, "Lord, I've been running away. I've tried to do this my own way. But now, I'm through. I'm ready to commit to you."

I stood up with a renewed focus and a fresh faith. I knew that I had found it. I had truly found what matters. And this time, I was sticking with it. It's funny to me that people associate Christianity with a boring life. For me, life *without* Christ was boring. *With* Him, it has been the greatest adventure I could've imagined.

Someone Is Always Watching

Although I didn't fully give my life to God until then, I never doubted His existence in it, especially during times of war. Even if I was discouraged, I never once thought that He had deserted me. I had a sense of security in His promise and a strong faith in His love and grace. Besides that, He had proved His existence time and time again.

He proved it by keeping my entire family alive through raids and treks for safety. Because of God, we were unharmed.

He proved it by keeping Mother and Christel alive during postwar times, an extremely difficult time to be pregnant. Once she was out of labor, Mother bled internally, and the doctors couldn't seem to stop it. She had a direct person-to-person blood transfusion twice, and because the blood didn't perfectly match, it put her body into shock. We all thought Mother was going to die, but thank God, she made it through. After three weeks, they released her from the hospital.

God also kept Mother, Dad, and Ursula alive on the train strafing on their way home from Haida. Many were killed, but because of God, they lived. He kept Dad from being taken from us, on more than one occasion: by the German government, by the Czech guards, and by the Russian soldiers. Because of God, our family remained together. He kept me alive through scarlet fever, as well as various other illnesses and injuries. Because of God, at eighty years old, I am still alive and well.

I never totally understood the miracle of my life until I had given it to Christ. He saved me from torture, injury, confusion, fear, and even death. In the midst of every trial, He was there. He saved me before I knew who He was. He loved me before I ever loved Him. Through all the trials I faced, I discovered that **God will stand with us through every season, as long as we fix our focus on what truly matters: the race, the purpose, the life that He has planned.**

I didn't understand it then, but this growing relationship with Christ served as a light, making the events of the darkest time of my life much more clear. It brought purpose to my pain. Someone had been watching over me, but He wasn't just watching over me for my own sake. He was keeping me alive for a special reason. He had a plan for me to fulfill, and He wanted me to discover it.

Where Passion and Purpose Meet

We all have dreams. Usually they're pretty big. So imagine those dreams, magnified indefinitely. Imagine a dream that is greater than You ever thought you could fulfill. That's how God's dreams are for us. That's how great our callings are, the place where our God-given passion and purpose meet.

I discovered my calling to ministry not long after committing my life to Christ the first time, at fifteen years old. It was at a service in West Berlin conducted by a guest pastor—the pastor at First Baptist Church in Dallas, Texas, at that time. After the service, I introduced myself to the pastor and told him that I had a desire for ministry. He told me that his secretary could get me into a Bible school in the States. I waited and waited but never heard back from her.

Since that didn't pan out, I decided to get out of Germany another way—through the World Baptist Alliance. They were providing funding for some young people eighteen years of age or older to vacate the country and take temporary farm jobs in Australia or Canada. I applied, along with my cousin, Günter. We were both accepted and left for Canada in late July of 1952, a few weeks before my eighteenth birthday. My parents threw an early birthday/send-off party for me, and then we were on our way.

Leaving Germany was tricky. Legally, as residents of East Berlin, we were supposed to stay in the East. That was the whole reason for the Berlin Wall, which came several years later. Many intelligent people—doctors, lawyers, and prominent businessmen—took off to West Germany because they believed they could build a better future there. And they were right.

It was going to be hard, but still, we wanted to go. Once we got the word from the alliance that someone could loan us our fare to Canada, we took off. We took a streetcar and a bus from East Berlin to West Berlin, and then we stayed in West Berlin for a few days. There, we exchanged our East German passport for a temporary West German passport, which was good only for a few weeks, so that we would have time to make arrangements to get onto the immigrant ship.

We finally made it to Canada via an immigrant ship, and I moved from job to job trying to make my life work. About five years into my time there, after rededicating my life to God on that cold concrete floor, I also rededicated myself to fulfilling my calling, the plan God had for me. At first I was nervous that I had missed it, that I had waited too long. Then I found the Scripture that says that God's gift and His call can never be withdrawn[5].

That's when I knew that it wasn't too late. God would still fulfill His purposes through me. It may not be as I had once thought, but His way would be better, more satisfying than any way I could have planned on my own.

I continued attending Immanuel Baptist while training with the Canadian Army at Camp Borden. It wasn't long before I met a young lady named Judy

---

[5] Romans 11:29

there. We began dating soon after we met. A couple of months later, I also connected with Youth for Christ, an organization dedicated to sharing God's love with teens worldwide.

In Barrie, the small city I was living in at that time, I saw a great need for young people to experience Christ the way I had. I wanted to help them, so I began a chapter of the organization there. I know people looked at me and thought, *This young guy thinks he's going to do something!* But I was determined. I asked local ministers from various denominations to form a board, and we got started.

Every other week, we put on rallies with various speakers. We'd rent out movie theaters on Sunday nights, and as many as six hundred people would show up, ready to hear more about this God that so loved them. That was a big deal for a city of about one hundred thousand people. The chapter became a tremendous success in our small city.

It was during this time that I realized my gift for bringing people together for a common purpose—a gift that would later help me find success in business.

I loved my time building this chapter because I knew that by helping other people meet God I was fulfilling my purpose. From then on, I was convinced that no matter what my career turned out to be, my calling was to reach people with the love of Christ. I wanted those around me to know the God that I knew. I wanted them to find what matters.

In 1957, not too long after I began my time with Youth for Christ, I was staying at a friend's house in

Barrie while on leave. Early one morning, the military police from the army camp showed up at the house. They firmly let me know that I was summoned to ship out to the Suez Canal. I quickly learned that the Egyptians had blocked the canal, which brought on what we know today as the Suez Crisis.

I immediately called the board and told them that they would have to pray and begin the search to find another leader. I reported to the camp to receive my necessary inoculations, which I had a bad reaction to and was placed in the hospital for five days. Once I was feeling a little better, I reported for deployment.

As I was getting on the gigantic army truck, preparing to be shipped out, my name got called.

"Reinhold Preik! You are not a Canadian-born citizen. We cannot use you. I'm sorry," the officer said.

Apparently, Canada was seeking to be a peacekeeper, so the force they were building was supposed to be a neutral one. They weren't allowing any foreigners, which meant that I was forbidden to serve. Although I am certainly in favor of serving my country, what normally would've been a letdown was actually a huge blessing. I knew that God was watching out for me and for all the youth that I had been working with. Because I could not serve, I was able to return back to Barrie and spend several more months strengthening the chapter.

Since that time, I've held several relief pastorates and accepted numerous traveling speaking engagements, but my professional life ended up taking a different turn. Still, never once have I doubted my calling, and never once have I stopped pursuing it.

The most fulfilling life is one in which we find our calling and pursue it relentlessly. **Everyone has a purpose to fulfill, and we can fulfill it right where we are. No one is ever too old, too broken, or too lost.** Take it from me; it once seemed I was all those things. **The key to a fulfilling future is not to be perfect. It's to stay focused on what matters.**

4
How Persistence Pays Off

You've Got to Be Sticky

"Rein." Jennifer is awake now. I pull up a chair for her beside me.

"Good morning. Isn't this beautiful?" I ask in a whisper.

She nods as she slides in beside me and breathes in the morning air. As I look at her, I feel an enormous wave of gratitude. How blessed I am to share this moment with her!

I grab Jennifer's hand, and we sit in the quiet for a moment. After a couple of minutes, the dialog begins. Quiet conversation quickly progresses into enthusiastic dreaming, as we discuss our hopes for these children. We imagine just how great their lives can become as they pursue their goals with relentless passion.

I may not know much about many things, but if there's one thing I do know, it's how to chase a dream and how to keep chasing it, even when you feel like giving in. Perseverance is an absolutely vital trait for any person fulfilling their purpose. I like to call it being sticky.

Like many young men, I had two main life goals: to build a beautiful, lasting marriage and family and to have a successful career. It wasn't easy. It took time, and it took work. Most of all, it took getting back up every time I fell. And there was a lot of that.

By the time I finished grade 10, the final grade in German public schools at that time, I was sixteen. It was 1951, and I was ready to pursue a career. My parents were like most parents postwar: they wanted us to earn a living before seeking out further education. They said it was more important to decide what to do for a living and then to go out and do it. That way, I could help to rebuild the economy after the war and begin to build a life for myself. School would follow whenever.

I gratefully accepted their advice, but deep inside, I wanted more. I was an honor student in my school and received encouragement from my teachers to pursue a career in chemistry, which was my best subject. They were convinced I could climb the ladder quickly with a little more education, so I applied to a school that would teach me the ins and outs of the business.

In Their Words

Rein had a deep love for chemistry, from his time as a student in Germany until he sold his company. More often than not, if we were looking for Rein in the office, someone would say, "You had better go check the lab!" And sure enough, he'd be there! I think that was his favorite place to be. Chemistry was

> *his passion. He was fascinated by the evolution of products and technology. Not only was he a great leader, but he also loved his craft and did it well. (Diana Hyunen, CFO, Chemcraft International)*

The system required me to attend school a few days a week and, the other days, to work for a company that agreed to serve as my sponsor. Through this system, I learned about the different parts of the factory and the manufacturing process. In one of my classes of about thirty students, we were broken up into study groups of seven or eight each.

We were each told to pick a name bearing one of the prominent leaders of our time, for example, "study group Lenin" or "study group Marx." I proposed to my study group that we name ourselves "study group Haevelman," after a well-known professor at the University of Berlin and an honored fighter for the revolution. This professor had known Einstein and had experimented with him before Einstein moved to the states.

The group agreed, so I went to visit him at his office at the university. I nervously knocked on the door, waiting for an answer. Nothing. Again, I knocked.

"Yes?" a deep voice called out.

For a moment, I forgot why I was there. "Oh, umm, hi, Professor Haevelman?" I stumbled.

"Yes?" he repeated.

I then went into my whole spiel, trying to convince him of why he should allow us to use his name for our group. Afterward, I took a deep breath and waited. Silence.

"Why, of course!" he laughed. "I'd be honored."

I was so relieved. I laughed with him, trying to pretend that I hadn't been a nervous wreck that whole time.

"Tell me about yourself," the professor continued.

"About . . . myself?" I was a little confused. He was the one who had accomplished so much. Why would he want to know about me? But still, I told him about my family, about my studies, and about my future plans and goals. Then he gave me advice. I couldn't believe I was sitting in the office of a man who had accomplished so much of what I had wanted to accomplish, and *he* was calling *me* by name.

I was grateful for the time I had with Professor Haevelman that day, but I never expected to hear from him again. One day, however, I received an invitation to his birthday celebration.

I knew this was a big deal, and that I had to attend. So I got ready, put on my best clothes, and brought the perfect gift: one of Dad's beautiful paintings. In one of our conversations that night, he encouraged me to continue my studies. He said that he would find a spot for me at the Institute of Planning, an academy that made plans for the country's economy. Working there would ensure my success throughout East Germany.

This was huge. Not many students, if any, had ever received an invitation like this from this highly accomplished professor. I was inclined to accept his invitation, when I discovered the catch: to join the institute, I would also have to join the Communist party.

> ### In Their Words
>
> *Chemistry was so natural for Rein. I had his Chemistry teacher years later, and he said Rein was the best student he'd ever had. This teacher laughed that he had even tried to stump Rein, but he never could! Rein used to love to conduct chemical experiments on the veranda of our home in Berlin. Sometimes things would blow up, but apparently he learned what worked! (Sigi Oblander, sister)*

I mulled over the idea for weeks. I knew this could be an invaluable opportunity. If I didn't accept it, would I find the success I was yearning for? If I did, I would still have to start from the bottom, but it looked promising.

After much consideration, as tempting as the offer sounded, I decided that I wouldn't take it. I just couldn't stand side by side with men who believed differently than I did and pretend to believe the same. Although I was not yet living completely for God, I knew there was no way that I could deny the existence of Someone who I was certain had been watching out for me. I couldn't even pretend that I did.

So I decided to take the tougher route. I decided, along with my cousin Günter, to escape Communist Berlin, move to Canada, and start from square one. Selling this idea to my family was tough, but I think

Dad had empathy for me wanting to build a better life and, eventually, Mom gave in.

They took Günter and me to West Berlin, and from there we took a plane to Bremen where we stayed at an overseas home designed for refugees who had no place to stay while they were waiting for their next step. From there, we went to Canada and were split up, working in different cities. In Canada, I would have to build a life on my own, without the help of anyone. It was then that I truly understood the phrase, "Sometimes the hardest thing and the right thing are the same."

Leaving my family was one of the hardest things I have ever done. I'll never forget carrying my suitcase to the airport, with Mother and my sisters crying the whole way. Even Dad let a tear or two slip out.

When I got to the overseas home, I received a card that read, *"Reinhold Preik. DP–Displaced Person."* This was not our official title, but that's what people called those who had no official passport, only a temporary one. And boy, did those words sting. Reading them caused waves of fear and dejection to sweep over me. It was almost as if they were looking at me straight in the face, saying, "You don't belong here." I felt lost, alone, and scared. I *was* a displaced person, traveling halfway around the world to pursue a dream. I knew no one, and I had nothing . . . nothing but the dream in my heart and a greater vision for my future.

I hugged my family, accepting their tearful good-byes and promises of prayers with gratitude. I held tightly to the little homemade gifts my sisters had brought me and struggled to fight back tears. As the plane took off for Bremen, I worked hard to convince myself that I was doing the right thing by leaving behind everything I knew for everything I had only dreamt of.

Thankfully, I stayed on board, and after a few moments, the plane rolled forward. I'm convinced that you never really understand the consequences and impact leaving home has on your life until years down the road.

I waved one final good-bye, wondering how long it would be before I saw my family again. I viewed this trip as a little road trip, a short vacation. I *never* dreamt it would be ten years. But one thing was for sure: whenever I did make it back, I was going to make sure I had *made it*. I wasn't going to come back empty-handed.

On the Move

I left Berlin ready to work. But I had to wait for a ship, so I lived in the overseas home in Bremen for a few weeks. Unlike some of the others, I had no time to waste. I was without any West marks at all. So I got a job shoveling coal at night. It was a tough job, as my sore back and legs and the terrible blisters on my hands proved each morning. The coal was ground to the point it felt like tiny rocks. We would then haul it with a big shovel from a cart into a truck. That job lasted for two weeks, and then we got passage on a converted submarine supply ship and were off to meet the farmers we would work for.

When I first stepped on the boat, I took a look around. This was going to be a long trip. Our ship was a small one and was sectioned off with about eight to ten people in each room. Each person was assigned a cot, which was really not much more than a mat. Before we left, some of the stewards offered jobs to the men aboard the ship. I accepted one working in the kitchen. The food was served cafeteria-style. Some people complained about it, but I was just glad to have some!

After I worked in the kitchen for a while, I worked in the gulley, putting in about four hours a day. I was thankful for the job because it made the days pass by more swiftly, although I would be lying if I said that I wasn't expecting pay for it. By the end of the trip, they paid me but only in cigarettes, which were no good to me since I wasn't a smoker. I was so disappointed that I just ended up giving them away.

One night, on the second night of a three-night-long storm, a loud bolt of thunder awakened me. Moments later, the waves tossed the boat just enough to throw me out of my cot, against the wall. I was terrified of what could happen. We were in a small ship, and that ship was not stopping motion. The railing of the ship was lined with people getting sick.

Everyone was advised to go to the front of the boat so that we didn't get drenched with water. It was both a frightening and somewhat disgusting sight to see. The sea continued to get rougher and rougher until the third day, when it finally calmed down. We continued our journey, sailing for eight days and eight nights altogether.

I couldn't have been more ready for the ship to dock when we made it to Quebec City. I was surprised when I got there and everyone spoke French—not English. My German-English dictionary would do no good for me now! We stayed in Quebec City a day or so, until our train arrived, and then we took that train for three days and three nights.

At every stop along the way, we would drop off a train car or two full of people, detach the cart, and continue on to the next city. Because our train was an immigrant train and not a regular-scheduled one, we often had to make extra stops in little towns to let the scheduled trains go by.

On those stops, we had fun walking around, looking into the windows of stores. I'd notice all the delicious cakes, breads, and sweets and would think back to our scarce family dinner table in Berlin. At this point, the idea of having enough to eat was still fairly new to me. I would watch people in restaurants, amazed that they could actually order whatever they wanted to eat *and* get enough to fill their stomachs.

There, coffee was only about ten cents a cup, but it was a luxury in Germany! Just the thought of buying a whole carton of juice and being able to have it all to myself was an exciting thought to me. The first time I went into a diner with a friend, I was in awe! I guess that's what happens when you grow up the way I did. You're the farthest thing from a picky eater.

Unfortunately, I didn't have much money to spend yet, so I found myself skipping dinner and sleeping on wooden benches more often than I'd liked! The title "displaced person" never felt more real. It was in times like this that I often wondered if I had made the right decision by leaving behind everything and everyone I had known and loved so much. I was in a strange country now, and I already missed my family. I started to imagine the holidays without them, and my heart ached. Over and over I had to repeat to myself, "Have faith. It'll work out."

Christmastime was the hardest. My family celebrated so differently in Germany than they did in Canada. We ate different foods and had different traditions. The first time I saw a Canadian Christmas tree, it was a month before Christmas Day. I couldn't believe it!

We were never allowed to see the tree until Christmas Eve. When we did, it was a big event. The tree always held real lit candles. As a family, we would gather around it, pray, sing, and thank God for His wonderful gift of Jesus. Then we would open our gifts and sit down to a meal. Oh, how I missed these traditions! I thought that if only I could have them one more time, I would never take them for granted again.

A New Home

On the third night of our train ride, we got to my stop: Edmonton. The nerves were at an all-time high as I unloaded my suitcase from the train.

I arrived at a farmhouse to find I had a little room off of the kitchen. My job was to collect the potatoes from the large machine that dug them up. Then I was to put them into buckets and into a ditch about four feet deep. Next, I would shovel dirt and straw over the ditch to keep the potatoes from freezing during the winter.

My job ended with the season, so at the end of my time working there, I went into town to figure out what to do. I walked the streets, trying to decide whether I should go back to the immigration house or try to find a place at the Salvation Army. The funny thing is that today, I often hear young people worrying about the rest of their lives. I wasn't even close to thinking about five or ten years down the road. All I wanted to do was figure out the next day. What would I eat? Where could I work? That's how life was then. You just looked for an opportunity and took it. Once you exhausted that opportunity, you looked for another.

Thankfully, as I walked along those streets, a man recognized me from a German-speaking Baptist church I had attended a few times while there, and he invited me to stay with him for a few days. He helped me find a permanent place to stay and got me a job in a foundry where we made covers for the manholes in the street. I lived in a boarding house with several roommates and was paid about sixty-five cents an hour, working forty-eight hours a week. That covered my fifteen-dollar room and board at the boarding house but didn't leave room for much else.

Next, I took a window-washing job, which paid eighty cents, at best. From there, I got a job at Saint Joseph's Geriatric Hospital, earning ninety dollars a month, plus all my meals. I'll never forget walking into the bland-looking building confident on the outside but incredibly anxious on the inside.

"I need a job." I told the nun at the front desk.

"Well, what can you do?" she asked me.

The women all looked at each other I'm sure wondering what in the world this tall young German boy wanted with a Catholic hospital, and why he was so confident he would get the job. But I persisted.

"I can do anything. Whatever needs to be done," I said.

They looked around again. I wondered if they could see my nervousness.

"Have you done this type of work before?" she asked.

"Ummm . . . well, no. But I believe I can do it." My voice started to shake a little.

"Okay, we'll give you a shot. Come report back here tomorrow at eight o'clock."

I thanked them, and as I turned around, a big smile spread across my face. I was going to be all right. The next morning, I showed up and reported to the nurse. I followed her around, and she showed me how to do my new job.

They put me in charge of taking care of the male patients—giving them their baths, helping them use the restroom, cutting their hair, and giving them shots. I worked in that hospital for about a year, and then because of my experience, I got hired at the university hospital in Edmonton. I made about double the salary working as an orderly there. I assisted the doctor in giving people insulin shots (or electric shock treatment), which was the type of therapy given to those who picked up a stress disorder from the war. I cared for many soldiers who had fought in Korea. I stayed at that hospital for about six months.

At the end of those six months, I heard of a job in the Yukon, working for Keno Hill, a large mining company about two hundred miles west of Dawson City. They offered a much better income than working in the city, but it was extremely isolated. I wanted to go, but I had to find a ride. One day, I was introduced to a man who was heading that way and caught a ride with him, on the basis of a fifty-dollar IOU.

It was a two-day trip, since it was one thousand miles from Edmonton. The roads were gravel, not paved, which made for a rough ride. At night, we could hear wolves howling. I was just praying that our car wouldn't break down!

When we finally made it to the Yukon, they settled me into a bunkhouse with three other guys. They handed me a hardhat, some boots and an emergency light and told me where to report to the next day. I was put on the first ten-hour shift.

That next morning, I reported to my station. As the elevator lowered me about six hundred feet underground and into the mine, I was shaking. I still remember trying to hide it from the other men on the crew.

"Hey, here's the new guy. Show him what to do," one of the workers called out to another.

The man showed me how to drill holes (about twenty feet deep) throughout the area, fill them with dynamite, and blast them. Then he showed me to how to operate a machine that would take out loose rock that was the result of the blast, whether it was metal or stones or worthless materials. Finally, I learned how to transport the useful materials to a lift, onto a little train, and then out.

During my time in the Yukon, 1956

It was harder work than I had ever done, working ten-hour shifts six days a week. It brought back memories of those tough days in postwar Berlin, chopping tree stumps in sub-zero weather. Once again, I reminded myself of the lesson I learned that day—to keep moving no matter what. With every dig, I was moving one step closer to the life I had been dreaming of.

I ended up staying in the Yukon a little less than two years. I made good money there—enough to finally pay back my travel from Germany and to buy my first car, a 1952 used Chevy. It was a four-door, had three gears, and I only paid $600 for it. I was beyond excited! I felt like I was finally moving up in the world. To get your driver's license back then, all you had to do was go to the liquor store in a town nearby called Mayo. It cost five dollars and didn't even require a test!

Although I was elated to have my license and my own car, there were a couple of downsides to driving in the Yukon. First of all, gas was expensive—about one dollar a gallon. Also, the rugged roads were a tough place to drive. It was a normal occurrence to drive by and see a car stuck in a ditch somewhere, with a wrecker truck pulling them out.

One time, after a heavy rain, I got stuck in the mud for hours. Another time, I turned the car over on its side. I took a girl on a date, and as I was taking her to see the camp I was living in, I lost control of the car. We were all right, and the car only got a few dents, but I was not happy. I *loved* that car.

It was also normal to carry a spare tire and gasoline with you in the cold months so that you could light the tire on fire for heat in case you got stuck. Most trucks were designed to operate in cold weather, but you still had to be careful, especially with the big trucks. You had to keep them running twenty-four hours a day, or else they probably wouldn't start up again. Also, you had to use a special grade of diesel fuel that would not gel in the cold.

Sometimes, it would get so cold outside that I would have to take my battery out and put it under my bed at night. Then I'd take it back out anytime I wanted to drive. I lived in the company staff house at the time, which was up on a hill. I would put the battery back in the car, give the car a little shove, put it into second gear, and wait for it to start rolling. It was so freezing there that nothing would turn. Once it started rolling, I would have to jump in and start the car.

Living in the Yukon redefined what I associated with the word *cold*. One winter night, I looked at the thermostat and it read, "Fifty degrees below zero." I knew I was in for an unusual winter. Even after winter, there was permafrost; so under the two or three feet of earth, there was still about six feet of frozen soil that never thawed out. When the prospectors were working, they could only dig so far because the ground was so hard to thaw. They would then have to start a fire in the hole they had made. Usually it was about six inches at a time. The process took a while.

While I was still working in the mines, I met some prospectors who invited me to visit them and see what kind of work they did. I went once and began going anytime I got a couple of days off from the mines. I wasn't paid; it was purely recreational.

We started out each job surveying the land. We'd look for certain types of rocks with a certain structure. Then when we found something that looked promising, we'd start digging with picks and shovels. Once we got any traces of metal, we'd take it to the assay lab to see if there was any silver in our sample. If there was, we would go to that little liquor store in Mayo and file a claim.

Because we were way out in the freezing wilderness, in order to supplement our food, we would often hunt for wild game such as moose or deer, skin it, and then haul it up into a tree so that the wolves wouldn't get it. It would freeze, so when we got hungry, we would retrieve it, saw a piece off, thaw and cook it, and then haul the rest back up the tree. That was probably the most fun part of the whole job!

I accepted this side job for the excitement, but I quickly found that *excitement* wasn't the word to describe trips like these. The men only worked on one or two sites a year since it was such a long process. Prospecting was a lonely job and a lonely life. I was thankful that it wasn't my main way of earning a living.

Working in the Yukon, 1956

After working in that mine for several months, I was offered a job in the assay office of the same company. Because I had experience with chemicals, I felt it was a perfect job for me. The job was to determine how much silver was contained in a drill sample. I knew it was less money, but it was better hours, so I thought it would be a good trade-off. I got the job, and I really enjoyed it.

Working in the assay lab, 1957

By the end of my two years of working in the mines, I had some money. So when my friends told me that the new place to be was Vancouver, BC, I drove the nine hundred miles there and visited the employment office seeking a job in the area. They told me about a position in Lake Louise working for the Canadian Pacific Railway. The job was driving a truck taking supplies back and forth from the train station to the hotel. I applied and soon found out that I had gotten the job. So the Canadian Pacific Railway sent me a train ticket, and I rode the six hundred miles to get there.

I stayed in a staff house, which was a much more enjoyable experience than when I had worked in the mines. There was always something fun going on! There were about six hundred young adults, mostly university students, who worked in the summertime since the hotel was only open from spring to fall. At least four hundred of those were girls, so we men were a bit outnumbered.

In order to drive these large commercial trucks in Canadian parks, I had to have a special license. I was required to take a test for this one, which left me a little worried that my driving skills would be found lacking. Sure enough, when test time came, they took me into the mountains, and I was told to drive through all the tiny roads. It was scary, and I did not do my best driving, but thankfully I passed!

That job was a taxing one, and I believe my roommate there must have been suffering from depression. I'll never forget eating dinner with a guy I worked with, when a friend ran up to us out of breath. Between gasps for air, he filled us in: my roommate had gone hiking on his day off. When he didn't come back, they went out looking for him and found him at the bottom of a cliff. They came back and searched his room, finding a note that confirmed their suspicion: He had committed suicide. We were shocked.

That job certainly was a tough one, but it still had its perks. The hotel I drove for was a five-star hotel, and I became great friends with the executive chef there. He was a Swiss national and an incredible cook. He often saved food for me, so I ate like a king my entire time there. Sometimes, I went into Banff with the truck to pick up goods and to do favors for him. For my birthday, he threw a party for me, with about twenty of our good friends. He cooked every kind of German food you could imagine. I felt like I was at home again!

Our typical schedule there was twelve days on and four days off. I spent my off-days from the hotel working for Brewster's, a company that gave horse-guided tours to tourists. I loved taking people out for rides on the trails. They always thought they didn't need a tour guide until they couldn't get the horse to go the way they wanted it to!

At Lake Louise, I learned how to ride an ice pick down a mountainside and made frequent visits to the Colombia ice fields. I also mountain climbed there. My favorite mountain to climb was Mount Temple, although it was tough, so I only had the opportunity to do it twice. The climb took pretty much the whole day. My time there left me with a ton of great memories. Sadly, because that job ended with the tourist season, I was there for six months, from spring through fall of that year.

My last job before settling down was a drilling job in the Rockies to help build the Trans-Canada Highway. I had operated a heavy drill in the mines, so I knew I could do the same on the Canadian mountainside. After I finished my job at the hotel, I drove to Banff and started the job in road construction. The workers there lived in a common staff house. I was shown to my room, which was fairly big. I had a few roommates, whom I did my best to fit in with, as we were a very diverse group of men. Meals were supplied by the local diner nearby. I'll never forget the fun evenings we spent enjoying each other's company in that diner.

The day after I arrived, I grabbed my hardhat and tools and reported to the project engineer who explained to me the operation of the large track mount drill. The whole way, I was asking myself, *Can I really work with these tough guys all day, every day?* It was an intense work schedule. The days were often rough and held a lot of responsibility.

The job in the Rockies only lasted from September to the end of November because by then, the road was frozen over with ice. After this job, I enlisted in the Canadian Armed Forces. I was placed in Camp Borden, serving there until the terrible swimming accident, which landed me on leave in Barrie.

It was now 1956. I was twenty-two years old, and I had spent about four and a half years in Canada. I was beginning to grow tired of working transient jobs. I started to wonder if I would ever fulfill the desires I had for a successful career as a paint chemist. Besides that, I didn't even have time to start thinking of building a marriage and family. But just when you think you're at a dead end, that's often when the miracle happens. That's when you find the break you are looking for.

With my second car, 1957

Settling Down

While I was a member of the Canadian Armed Forces, I built the Youth for Christ chapter in Barrie. One day, I got news they were planning to transfer me out of Camp Borden, which meant I would have to leave Barrie and the Youth for Christ chapter I had built there. That concerned the board of the chapter because they felt there was no one to take my place at that time.

They wanted me to stay, but I told them the only way that could happen was if I was out of the army. So they applied for a discharge with the military officials. I was then granted an honorable discharge and began to focus solely on the chapter. Because it wasn't a paying job, it wasn't long before I realized my need to make money. I knew it would be tough to lead the chapter and work a paying job, but I also knew that I needed to try.

My first effort was with a man from church who had an agency for vacuum cleaners. I worked as a salesman for him to support myself as I continued to build the Youth for Christ chapter. I did this for about a year. After a while, I started feeling guilty for selling people a product for a premium price that I wasn't sure they could afford. Plus, my girlfriend Judy and I had been dating several months now, and we decided that we wanted to marry. I wanted something that would be stable enough for us to build a life around.

That's when I quit my job at the vacuum cleaner agency and searched for a career to invest in. The board searched for someone to replace me at the Youth for Christ chapter and found a Welsh Bible school grad that seemed like the perfect fit to take my place. I then secured a position at a large paint company in Toronto. They offered me a position as a research technician in the polymer department. I accepted, and Judy and I married and moved into an apartment in Toronto.

I worked hard at this job and did well. I was granted a few patents in the polymer area, which was not the norm for someone my age and with my amount of formal education. We had saved enough money to rent an apartment and buy a car, and I was feeling pretty good about our financial stability. Not that we were wealthy by any means, but we were able to make the payments on what we had. I also fulfilled my heart for ministry by getting heavily involved in the Fellowship Baptist Young People's Association in Toronto.

During that time, Judy and I decided that we wanted to start building a family. It wasn't long before she got pregnant with our son Marc. Those first-time parenting thoughts definitely took their toll on me at first.

Will I be a good dad? Can I provide for another person? What if he doesn't like me?

The few weeks leading up to Judy's due date, I was a nervous wreck. However, once I held that little baby boy in my arms, it was as if all my worries faded away. I had never felt a love like this before. I knew I wouldn't fail at taking care of him. I couldn't.

Judy took her maternity leave, but when the time came to go back to her position at PPG Industries, she was more than ready. Because we were both extremely busy during this time, my sister Sigi flew over from Germany to take care of Marc while we were at work. She was only seventeen years old at that time, and after about eight months, she decided she was ready for something a bit more challenging.

While she was with us, she met and became close friends with a girl from Sweden. This girl had gotten involved with a man who abused drugs, and it got so bad that the drug pushers tried to involve her as well. She wanted to detach herself from him, so she went back to Sweden, and Sigi went with her. After Sigi left, we bought our first house in Aurora, about twenty-five to thirty miles north of Toronto. It was a semidetached house, and I paid $11,800 for it with a $1,500 deposit.

I worked for the paint company there about five years. One day, I heard about a new business that was being started by several of the men who used to work in the company. They were operating out of Cornwall, Ontario, which was only a few-hour drive from us. Because of my limited formal education—I didn't have a university degree—I didn't see myself moving much further with my current employer, so I applied with this startup business. I received an offer to work as a coatings chemist, accepted it, and moved Judy, Marc, and myself to Cornwall.

I worked in that lab for several years. During my time there, I wanted to make sure I wasn't neglecting the assignment I felt God had given me years before, and I also wanted to better equip myself for what I believed the future held. So in 1962, I made the decision to leave the company to move back to Toronto and attend Toronto Bible College. The owner of the company thought I was crazy, but it was something I felt I had to do.

We moved, and Judy started working again for her former employer, while I studied and looked after Marc. After I finished several semesters of school in Toronto, I decided to complement my studies at a Bible school in Germany. That would give me the opportunity to continue learning, to see my family after ten years of absence, and to introduce them to Judy and Marc.

This was the first time I had been back since I'd left, and it was the first time my family was able to meet my own new little family. Judy and Marc stayed with

Mother and Dad while I went to classes. Watching my parents with their grandson gave me so much joy.

After finishing up my studies there, I was prepared to get involved in the ministry. However, I needed to make money for my family, and I just didn't understand how to do that in ministry at the time. We had a few supporters whom we were thankful for, but the donations were not enough to keep us going. So I decided to move back to Cornwall and continue to work for my previous employer. It was hard to leave my family again, especially because Marc was now so in love with his grandparents.

Upon my return to Cornwall, I continued working in the lab. However, it didn't take long for me to realize that the real earning potential was in sales and technical service. I worked hard to convince the owners to let me go on service calls. They agreed, and from there, I got assigned a territory, which meant that I had to move about three hundred fifty miles away from the plant to Hanover, Western Ontario.

About this time, Judy and I started trying to have another child. We were saddened when we found out that Judy could no longer conceive because of a serious health problem. So we adopted our beautiful baby girl, Krista, who was only six months old at that time. I loved everything about adoption, and I loved everything about my new little girl. She was such a light to my life! I am unbelievably grateful for the process of adoption because without it, I would have missed out on one of God's greatest gifts to me—my beautiful daughter, Krista.

The truth is that we're all adopted. Before Jesus's time, if you weren't a Jew, you couldn't be a part of His family. Our adoption papers were made available when God sent His only Son Jesus to die for our sins. With that gift, He made us His own. Just like Krista became a part of the Preik family, so we all become a part of God's family. What a beautiful picture of grace!

My daughter, Krista, and her two children, Justin and Kristen

While living in Cornwall, I had the freedom to travel because of my job in sales. So on the weekends, when I had time, I would speak in churches nearby. Eventually, I was asked to pastor a full-gospel country church just a few miles outside of Hanover. All this was a strenuous schedule, but I loved it. I felt I was finally pursuing my purpose, and at the same time, I was meeting my career goals. Mother and Dad even visited once, and I could tell that they were proud of all that I had accomplished. Seeing their pleased faces made me want to work even harder.

It seemed I was on the road to having it all, but I soon realized I was missing one thing—a healthy marriage. After ten years, my relationship with Judy began to deteriorate; and one day, after a couple of years of trying hard to make it work, she presented me with divorce papers. I was absolutely crushed.

Immediately, I began questioning myself. What did I do wrong? Was I not paying enough attention? Did I not love her enough? But as with most breakups, one day you realize, there's nothing left you can do but move on. I still had a beautiful little family I had to focus on caring for.

After everything was settled in court, I was given the responsibility to look after Marc and Krista. I had to represent a company, deal with the heartache of my divorce, and try hard to care for two small children. I was broken, but honestly, what hurt the most was that with the divorce from my wife came what felt like a divorce from my purpose.

I had been taught that if a man couldn't lead his home, he couldn't lead a church. Today, it seems people have more grace on those in similar situations; but back then, in my case, it was different. **We must always be careful what we teach people about how God's grace works. It could drastically alter the course of their life.** It did mine. I gave up my work with the churches I had been preaching in and stuck to working on my role as a father.

I'll never forget taking a walk in a snowstorm late one night thinking to myself, *If I never came back, that would be all right. The kids would be better off without me.* Of course that wasn't true, but when you're in a desperate time, you can almost convince yourself of anything. I prayed to God, and He reminded me that He had never left me before, and He wouldn't now. God will always remain close to the brokenhearted. He will rescue those whose spirits have been crushed.[6]

Climbing the Ladder

When I first returned from Germany, I had been pleased to see that the company had grown some during my time away. Throughout the months that passed, it continued to grow; and as it became more successful, so did I. After a couple of years of being back with the company, first in the lab and then in sales, they had an issue with the technical director. I was asked to take over his position and move back to Cornwall. So I did.

---

[6] Psalm 34:18

After a few years as the technical director, the position of general manager was offered to me; and two years later, I became the president of the entire company. Now, I was the one responsible for growth and profits. By this point in time, I was financially stable. I had a different struggle though, and it bothered me to no end. I had two children at home with no parent to spend much time with them. I was gone all day, constantly working hard to provide well for our family.

I was a little depressed, and my family must have heard it in my voice when I called them every so often from Canada. After a while, my sister Christel decided that she would move her family to Canada to be there for me and to help me with the children. One November, I sent her a plane ticket; and by February 1, 1969, she arrived with her family. I had never been more thankful for my sister than I was during that time—for her help and for her presence in my home. Having her there reminded me of the home I grew up in. It reminded me of the kind of family I wanted to build.

Christel helped me during the day. It was incredible having her there, but she had her own family to take care of at night, so I still needed someone then.

One day, a young woman by the name of Ethel came in to help. She would cook dinner, clean, and help with the chores. I was grateful for her help. I thought she was very sweet and that she was helping to keep my family together. Ethel and I dated for a few months, and then we married.

We lived in Cornwall and had three children there: Quentin, Austin, and Curtis. It was a bit of a peculiar position leaving Cornwall with Judy and then later living there with Ethel. People didn't know what had happened, and some didn't understand. Although it hurt me, I had to let the comments and stares roll off my back. I focused on the friends I had who were supportive of me and of my decisions and on working hard to take care of my family.

During that time, I filled pulpits for pastors while they were away, but I didn't feel as connected to my calling as I once had. The pain of my failed marriage still haunted me. From the outside, it seemed I had it all: a beautiful family, a nice home, several sports cars, a boat, the works. However, I felt I had lost what mattered most—the church and my ability to pursue my calling in the ministry. But thank God, He works everything out for the good of those who love Him and who continue after His purpose.

My sons: Austin, Quentin, Curtis, and Marc at my seventieth birthday party, 2004

Building from Scratch

With the pain of regret still fresh in my heart, I decided to turn my focus toward what I could do something about: my career. I had stayed with the company I was at for fifteen years (except for that sabbatical in Germany) before I strongly sensed a desire to start my own. I learned about a solvent supplier in the chemical industry who was looking for a partner to go into the coatings business with. We met and agreed that we wanted to form a company. I would begin with 25 percent equity, and they with 75 percent. This new company would operate out of the facility the majority partner already owned. We named the new company Chemcraft Systems.

My family and I packed up yet again and moved to Port Hope. After only six months with our new company, something completely unforeseen to me happened. The majority partner of Chemcraft went bankrupt. I was in shock. I went to the bank to speak with the receivers and learned that the company's engineering and process was faulty, resulting in low product yield, thus the financial losses.

The company had no other option but to shut down. But I wasn't about to let my dream be thrown away with the bankruptcy, so I talked to Don, a friend whom I had enjoyed working with at that solvent company. We decided to continue Chemcraft together, each owning 50 percent of the company. There was just one problem: our operating facility was still inside of the bankrupt solvent company's property.

Don and I made a deal with the bank. We purchased the company's assets, taking on some debt, and they gave us the title to their property, including their emptied-out facility. I now owned 50 percent of the company, and he owned 50 percent of it. This was a great partnership. Don and I got along well, and I enjoyed working with him.

I was excited but realistic. We were a small company who started with only four employees. I worked in the lab, in production, and at times, even in delivery. I quickly learned that the first million dollars in sales is the hardest. But the hard work paid off, and we grew into a multimillion dollar company within only a few years.

As we grew larger, our competition became greater. After a couple of years, we had seen considerable growth. Our market share in the industry grew, but we had to work hard for every bit of business. I suggested to Don that we also partner with a European company in order to obtain new technology, but the proposed pairing went against his religious beliefs. He was a member of a church that had convictions about being unequally yoked in business with an unbeliever. I respected his convictions; however, I knew this would be a tough thing to avoid if we wanted to reach our goal of dealing with a public company. And Don did too.

So he proposed an agreement that allowed us to go ahead with the acquisition of the new technology. That proposal was to split the existing company into two separate operations. Don would hold real estate, and I would continue with Chemcraft as the operating company. I then owned 100 percent of Chemcraft, which allowed me to seek other technology partners.

We continued like this for a few years, until the company grew to the point that I had the financial strength to purchase the real estate from Don. It was unusual that we conducted these dealings with no conflict, but I am so glad that we did. Don and I remained friends for a long time, and we always had a tremendous amount of respect for each other.

Hard work always pays off. When you're faithful with the little that you have, just like I was with my 25 percent, you will be entrusted with more. So much more that you can't even contain it all!

Two Is Better Than One

Just like in life, in business, connections are a big deal. Partnerships can make or break you. You've got to surround yourself with people who won't try to sabotage your dream but who will attach to it, helping you to make it a reality.

After Don exited from Chemcraft, we negotiated with a Danish company in a similar position to us who was looking into getting into the Canadian and U.S. markets. We decided that we wanted to partner with them and discussed the terms: they would supply technology, and we would take care of everything else. This was a good deal for us because their technology was advanced compared to what was then available in Canada, so we agreed. They made a financial investment and in return owned 40 percent of the corporation. From then on, business increased rapidly. Because of our expansion into the foreign marketplace, we renamed the company Chemcraft International.

In the matter of a few years, Chemcraft became the largest private operating company in the industrial wood finishing business. We decided the next logical step was to move into the United States because if you want to be truly strong in Canada, you have to be strong in the United States.

During my search for a U.S. company, I found a Winston Salem company that was available. We felt this acquisition could really take the business to the next level. However, since the Danish company owned the technology and had funds available, they insisted that they bring their own manager from Denmark. I agreed reluctantly and accepted 20 percent of the U.S. company.

After they operated the company for two years, they experienced considerable financial losses, and the business in the United States ended up not being profitable. So I suggested we merge the Canadian operation with the U.S. operation at the same ownership level we had originally entered into.

We would take over all financial losses and in return obtain ownership of all Danish technology. The Danish company would still own 40 percent of our company, and we would own 60 percent of it and continue to run its day-to-day business. We would also own 100 percent of the U.S. company, taking on their debt and gaining control to make decisions that we felt needed to be made.

They agreed. We became dominant in Canada and started making a name for ourselves in the United States as well. The partnership worked out, and Chemcraft continued to grow.

Then another unforeseen event occurred. After a few years of successful operation, a Swedish company bought the Danish company. After we finally got used to working together, a Dutch company bought the Swedish company and complicated things for us yet again. This time, it presented a problem for us since the Swedish company owned a competitor of ours in the United States, a situation that simply could not occur in our business. So we approached them, made a deal, and bought back the 40 percent of Chemcraft.

After this, I wanted to ensure that the company would continue with a strong, committed team. So I invested 25 percent of the company into the key employees. They would have a combined ownership of 25 percent of the company, and I would own 75 percent of it. This kept the morale strong, as people felt a new sense of responsibility and allegiance to Chemcraft. After all, they were now part owners.

In Their Words

Rein was like a general–standing at the forefronts to forge ahead and make ideas happen. Over the years we worked on organic growth, but one of his goals was to become global. He started in Ontario, Canada, and then made joint ventures across Canada. He led the acquisition of the American companies,

> *and then gained representation in Europe, Singapore, and Brazil. It was continually evolving.*
>
> *Rein is an incredible visionary to start with something so small and to have the focus to grow a company into something that we are all very proud of. He does that with everything he is a part of. (Diana Hyunen, CFO, Chemcraft International)*

Chemcraft continued to grow from there. By this time, we had over five hundred employees present in several markets in Canada, the United States and Brazil, a minority partnership in Singapore, with plants in China and Vietnam. We had different reasons for each partnership, making sure each one was continually beneficial to the company and to our customers.

For example, we started our plant in Brazil because at one point, the Brazilian government decided they needed more labor content in their country. They made a rule that only 50 percent of the products purchased could be taken as raw, and the rest had to be finished in the country and then exported. That was a problem for us because a lot of our customers bought raw logs to process and cut for flooring and other products. We got that plant in Brazil so that we could keep those customers.

Partnerships like this one began occurring more frequently, so I started traveling often, working hard to keep in contact with all our plants. Business was expanding, but once again, things were not so great on the home front. After fifteen years of marriage, one day I came home to divorce papers sitting on my side of the bed.

I had known things were headed for disaster this time, and I had tried everything I could think of to make it work. I hope you never judge someone who has been through a divorce because you never know how hard they tried. Sometimes, there's just nothing you can do. Sometimes, even persistence reaches its limit.

Life is kind of like an algebra problem: when you make one wrong decision, it affects the next one and the next one, until you end up with an answer you weren't looking for. I certainly made some decisions that I'm not proud of throughout my life, but thankfully, I serve a God who redeems, restores, and gives new beginnings. And that's just what I asked Him to do.

New Beginnings

By the time of my second divorce, I was forty-eight years old. I had achieved one of my two dreams. I owned a successful business, but I was obviously struggling on the relational side. It seemed I could only handle one at a time.

One night, I knelt by my bed and prayed the same prayer I had prayed so many years before, as a young man who felt he had no direction.

I said, "God, I've been trying to do things my own way again. Please take control."

He did. It wasn't long after my divorce that I met Jennifer. She was working in sales for a company we bought out in North Carolina when our paths crossed. We began dating, and I got to know her and her sweet little ten-year-old girl, Erin. I started to picture a life with them and what a beautiful life it could be. After a few months, I proposed to Jennifer, she accepted, and a few months later, my sister Sigi married us.

With Jennifer on our wedding day, July 1, 1987

In Their Words

When I think of Rein and my mom, I think of that saying, "Behind every great man is a great woman." My mom is behind the scenes and always so supportive of him. I appreciate the role model that they set for me. (Erin Lee, daughter)

With Jennifer, hiking in Banff, 2000

For about twenty-seven years, I finally enjoyed both dreams-come-true at the same time—a thriving business and a wonderful marriage to a beautiful woman. Letting God fully take control was the best decision I ever made. He can direct you through any wilderness and out of any tough spot you have made for yourself.

I was seventy-two years old when I knew that I had gone as far as I wished to go on the business front. It was time for me to sell Chemcraft. We let the bank know to put out the word in the industry, and several buyers placed their bids. We sifted it down to our final options and set up a meeting to consider our decision.

I'll never forget that morning, sitting inside a conference room in Winston Salem. The bigger the company gets, the more structured it gets, so this meeting was one of the most organized, controlled meetings I'd ever been a part of. The buyers sat on one side; our head staff on the other. My COO sat two seats down from me. During the meeting, he received an unsolicited offer through e-mail to his smart phone. He interrupted, leaned over, and whispered to me, "I just got this e-mail. You have to read it."

It seemed inappropriate to me to be reading an e-mail in the middle of such an important meeting. But I did, and I'm so glad I did! That message was from a representative of a company that we had previously been in business with. They were offering 40 percent more than the other bids we received. It was the same company we had merged with years before! We made the deal, and neither of us could have been happier. They were happy because we had excellent standing in the industry, and we were happy because we got a premium price.

When we entrust our decisions to God, it's amazing how He'll pull through. He'll cause everything to work out for the best if we will work hard and leave the results up to Him.

Life requires us to stay in the race. In a culture of get-up-and-go, it requires us to stick with things. Sometimes, we fall. Sometimes, we feel stuck. But if we hold in there, we find that persistence really does pay off.

> ### In Their Words
>
> *In 2007, Rein made the decision to consider selling the company for several different reasons. I think it was difficult for him because he was extremely loyal to and protective of all of his employees. Some of the biggest chemical companies in the world wanted to buy it, but he was careful because although he knew it was time to sell, he wanted a legacy to be created. (Diana Hyunen, CFO, Chemcraft International)*

5
How to Turn Weaknesses into Strengths

Making Negatives Your Positives

Jennifer and I finished our conversation just as we were sipping our last bit of coffee.

"Isn't it amazing?" she asked.

"Isn't what amazing?" I replied.

"This. The fact that we're here. The fact that two once very broken people are now helping to fix something, to fix someone. It just doesn't seem like it should happen."

I sat and thought for a moment. She was right. I never thought a young man once living in poverty would ever have the opportunity to help financially with such large projects or that a man who was once labeled a "displaced person" could ever help others to find a home.

But that's how life is, you know. Sometimes weaknesses actually turn out to be strengths. Sometimes disappointments spark a hope for something greater, and setbacks reveal opportunities for advancement.

"That's what these children need to know," I thought. They need to understand that what was meant to harm them can be used to help, if only they'll keep their perspective right, even when it looks *difficult. When you're in the midst of a problem, it's hard to see the good. But it's always there.*

Life is a journey composed of hills and mountaintops. There are some great and some not so great days, weeks, months, and sometimes even years. But if there's one thing that leading a business has taught me it's this: **we have the power to turn our greatest liability into our greatest asset. It's all in the perspective and approach.**

I relearned this lesson many times. One of them was in 1978, right after our company had joined with the Danish company. We started Chemcraft in 1976, so we had only been going for a couple of years when a fire broke out in the plant. There was a weigh tank that measured material electronically, and it fed into a mixing vessel. In order to prevent a fire, that tank needed to be grounded by static lines. Some of the workmen had not clamped them securely enough, and the liquid began to create static. Before we knew it, volatile solvents mixed with some nitrocellulose and had started a huge fire.

When the fire alarm rang loudly throughout the plant, my heart started racing. I knew how dangerous chemicals could be. I jumped up and ran out the back door of my office, praying under my breath the whole way. Sure enough, there they were—flames billowing out of the windows. I stood there for a few moments before coming to my senses, watching hundreds of thousands of dollars' worth of equipment go down the drain. Behind me, police cars and fire trucks sped in, closing down the eastbound lanes of Highway 401, the highway our plant was near. The smoke was so thick; it would've surely caused trouble for those driving by.

Thankfully, they closed off the lanes and put out the fire just in time. I was relieved to find that no one was hurt but was devastated when I realized that we had pretty much lost everything. I'll never forget trying to calm my racing thoughts as I ran to our supply building, made sure the fire doors were sealed to the adjacent warehouse, and directed people to spray water on the places where the most flammable materials were stored. As they went back and forth putting the fire out, my mind flooded with thoughts of fear and worry.

What are we going to do?
Am I going to lose all that I've worked for?
How will I care for my growing family?

This time, I could clear my mind, though; and as I had learned to do in so many instances before, I turned the situation over to God. Time and time again, I had found that things worked out much better when left in His hands. I settled down and assured myself, *If everything is gone, I will just find a job making enough money to care for my family by working for someone else.*

Thankfully, we didn't lose everything, and although I didn't know it then, that "setback" was about to become one of Chemcraft's greatest opportunities for advancement. Once the damage was assessed, we received some money from our insurance company, but it was only a couple of hundred thousand dollars, not enough to operate at the capacity at which we normally operated. We had to look for other options.

The fire at Chemcraft, 1976

The one building on our land that didn't get burned down was the warehouse, which was attached to the plant. The only reason it didn't was because of the fire door that had been shut just in time. That meant we had about a month's worth of finished goods stored up that we could sell. I had a plan, but I wasn't sure that it would work.

I went to the customers and explained our situation. I asked them to buy our entire inventory and pay for the products right away, in cash, rather than placing orders in a timely matter. We needed to rebuild immediately and needed to empty out that warehouse so that we could convert it into a production space. Many of them were gracious enough to comply, and we managed through that fire without losing a single customer. On top of that, we rebuilt the plant much better than it was before.

From then on, business matured consistently. I could say it was chance that I had good customers who stood with me. I could say I was lucky to have lost the plant so that we could realize our potential for a better one. But that's not what I believe. I believe that what started out as a setback turned into an even greater comeback because we kept our perspective right. We kept it positive, focusing on what we could do rather than growing upset over what we couldn't do.

It was obvious that we couldn't go back in time and clamp the static line right to avoid the fire. We couldn't go back in time and put it out sooner. But we could utilize our best resource—the people we had built relationship with—our customers. We focused on what we could do, and it brought us through to an even greater place than before.

This happened again and again throughout my career. It also happened the time the company I initially partnered with went bankrupt. What I first saw as a tough time was actually an opportunity for me to begin my own company, a lifelong dream of mine. When I thought I was losing everything, I had to shift my perspective: Everything *was* being taken away, but it was so that I could receive even more.

Bad things are going to happen. That's just the way it is. Life is not comfort or steadiness. It's sometimes turmoil and always change. But no matter how negative the situation, we can always find something positive to focus on.

When Less Is More

"Less is more" is not a concept most of us like to think about. The majority of people are drawn to more—more money, more power, more influence. But in business, it's proven itself to be true time and time again: you have to be willing to give up, to have less, in order to get more. It's the principle of investing. Of course, it doesn't work out perfectly every time. As we all know, every investment doesn't make a great return. Rewards require risk. But you certainly can't receive more without giving something up.

I fell in love with racing as a young boy. I had watched my friends racing their bicycles and asked my parents if I could have one. We couldn't afford it, so Mother said no. It was a wonderful surprise when one day, Dad came home with an old track bike he had bought on sale from the shop in town. It had wooden rims that ran inside of small tracks.

I was ecstatic. I went straight to the track and began training. I was naïve then, letting the adrenaline convince me that I could do anything. I soon found out that adrenaline isn't the best guide when I ended up wrecking that first day, leaving both my body and my pride hurting. We couldn't afford another bike, so

I had to wait until years later to indulge my need for speed. When I did, I moved onto cars.

Driving my Ferrari, 2005

In 1990, I joined a Porsche club and began racing on the weekends. I later decided to attend the Porsche Sport Driving School for instructors so that I could teach people high speed driving. Around 1995, I also joined a Ferrari club. Then I joined a private club that had retired race car drivers such as Paul Newman driving in it. I have driven many different kinds of cars at high speeds on many different tracks. It doesn't matter what car, which track, or how many times I've done it; it never gets old to me. I absolutely love high-speed driving.

Getting ready to go racing, 2005

At the Porsche delivery center in Germany, 1996

Although I enjoy them, it's not necessarily the cars I drive or the people that I meet that make me want to go back to the track every time. It's the rush I get as I'm speeding around a turn, the risk I take when I get down into that seat, clasp my helmet on, and rev up the engine. I can't get enough of it.

As a businessman, I know that that risk, that rush of adrenaline, shows itself in more than just racing. There were plenty of times I felt the same feeling when making an important decision for Chemcraft. That's because just like in racing, in business, there are risks to be taken. **You'll never win if you're not first willing to take the track.**

That's not to say that we should go out and make irrational decisions because that's not risk; that's just immaturity. Risk still requires a certain amount of trust. You don't want to invest in the stock of a company you have not built at least a little trust in, one that you believe is going to do well.

This is why I keep my trust in God and allow Him to lead me. Then when I take a risk, I know that even if it doesn't turn out the way I imagined it would, it will still work out for the good. I've found that He will always turn my weaknesses into strengths and my less into more.

Growing up, we had a coal chute in our house. My sister Sigi would stand at the top of it, and my Dad would yell for her to jump to him.

"But I can't see you!" Sigi would yell out of desperation.

"That doesn't mean I'm not here," Dad would reply.

When we're weak or facing a disappointment, just because we don't see the silver lining yet doesn't mean it's not there. Just because we don't see God working doesn't mean He's not. He is. That's why we've got to keep our perspectives fixed on the positive. Then our bad will turn into good, and our good will turn into great. Our weak will turn into strong, and our strong will turn into unbreakable.

Jennifer and I at the presentation given by my staff for my twentieth anniversary at Chemcraft in Canada, 1996

A painting of me by Bruno Lord, 1996

Jennifer and I at the Chemcraft twentieth anniversary party, 1996

When I'm Weak, He Is Strong

It's up to us to shift our perspective to see the good in a situation, but sometimes, God will allow us to experience a situation that makes it hard *not* to change it. That situation often comes before we ever even realize we need a shift. That's what happened to Jennifer and me in the fall of 2010. Jennifer had gone into the doctor's office for a regular mammogram, assuming she would just get in, get out, and get on with her day. But the doctor's response stopped her right in her tracks.

"I see a couple of things. I'm going to need to biopsy them," she said.

Jennifer's heart sunk. As she sat there, she just kept thinking, *This can't be me. This can't be me!* But it was, and we were scared. For the next few weeks, we prayed and kept our hearts set on the promises we found in God's Word. A few weeks later, she went back in for a checkup, and they told her that there was a tumor, but it was self-contained and was not on her lymph nodes. It was a stage zero, which meant it was at the safest stage possible. She had to go through chemo treatments, but she came out just fine.

Obviously, people who fight cancer have it a lot worse than we did. We were blessed that our fight wasn't a long one filled with as much pain and heartache as is often the case in cancer stories. But even in those few weeks of waiting and throughout those months of chemo treatment, it was tough. We weren't sure what the rest of our lives would look like or how much longer Jennifer's would be.

No matter who you are or what you do, until you receive news like that, you never feel that you might not be on earth tomorrow. Death had never felt so real for Jennifer as it did the day she received that terrible report. Still, there was a positive in it all. During those weeks, we did a lot of soul searching that brought an awakening to our hearts. It was as if God was saying, "You've got to make the rest of your life count for something. I've made you for more."

We both emerged from that experience with a strong sense of purpose. Our perspective on life in general changed drastically, pushing us to pursue our passions with greater determination. That's when we started working with both Love Botswana and Journey Church, two organizations we love and believe in so much. We felt privileged to have such a great part in their development.

Now, it's hard to imagine our lives without the blessings that this scare ultimately brought into them— the people, the projects, a new, healthier lifestyle, and the zeal for living each day with purpose. Today, every day feels like a blessing. Every day feels like an opportunity to make our lives count. God's hand was definitely on us during that time, and we still feel it every day. When an experience is forced upon you like it was on Jennifer, it will change you.

It's Not Always What It Seems

On days when I feel like letting a negative perspective take over, I think back to war days, specifically the dreadful trip from Haida back to Berlin. When we finally made it across the border and into Dresden, we were shocked to find the city, once so beautiful and world renowned for its fine china, now completely in shambles. It appeared to us that there was hardly a building standing.

Just five months earlier, in February, it had been destroyed in one U.S. Air Force and two Royal Air Force raids. Nearly one hundred thirty-five thousand people had been killed in two days alone. Even months later, people were still scraping and digging through the rubble to find anything usable, such as a pair of worn shoes, a piece of cloth, or a pot. It was a desperate time.

As we walked through the city, our bodies grew even more tired and weak. We were supposed to take a boat the rest of the way into Berlin, and we were all looking forward to the rest. But when we got to the designated place for loading, we saw hundreds of others waiting for the same. We asked what was going on and found that we had just missed the boat. There wouldn't be another one coming for a week.

We were discouraged. Now what would we do? We had no food, no shelter, and no money. Just as we were trying to figure it out, a woman walked up to Mother out of the clear blue and asked if we needed a place to stay. Mother told her that we did, and she let us stay with her for that entire week. We were grateful to have a place to rest and food to eat.

Still, we were frustrated that we'd missed our transportation into Berlin. After such a long journey, we were ready to be home. We were anxious to discover the condition of our house and to see how Opa and Oma were holding up, if they were even still alive. But Mother and Dad encouraged us over and over again to keep our attitudes positive.

A couple of days later, we found out that the very boat we missed had been stopped, and some of the people had been loaded onto freight cars and sent to the Soviet Union. The Russian government's goal was to get certain people to their country, specifically those working in the scientific field, such as chemists, physicists, and engineers. There they would question them about their work. We had heard plenty of horror stories about the way people were mistreated while there. Since Dad was an engineer, that could have very well happened to him.

We could not have been more relieved. That delay had been for our good. We were protected when our lives could have been lost. When we were so discouraged, thinking that we were missing our ticket to safety, God had another way planned for us that was much better.

It's just like the Bible says. God's thoughts are always greater, and His ways are always higher. He sees the end from the beginning, and He knows just what it's going to take to get us from where we are to where we need to be.[7] If we will trust Him, keeping our perspectives right even when everything else seems to go wrong, He will lead us into safety and blessing every time.

Making the Most of Your Position

Sometimes we get put in a position that we don't want to be in. It's not unusual; it happens to everyone. It's in those times that we've got to believe there's a reason for it and strive to make the most of where we are. My family was very fortunate throughout the war. We only lost my cousin, who contracted tuberculosis in a concentration camp and died. They picked him up because he had been a part of the Youth Movement in the Third Reich. Everyone else came out fine, although we had some close calls.

One of those close calls was an uncle who was fighting with the German Army in Russia. When the German Army invaded the city, they took over most of the commercial operations and put several of their own, most respected men in charge. Because of the skills my uncle had learned as a young man working in public life as a master miller, the Germans put him in charge of a flour mill in the city.

Later on, after the Germans retreated and he returned to Germany, the Russian security officers came back seeking revenge. They searched hard for anyone who had been a German officer. Because he was a manager of that flourmill, they found him, took

---

[7] Isaiah 55:9

him, and put him in one of their concentration camps in Siberia.

There were no Bibles or Scriptures to be found anywhere throughout the camp. However, my uncle knew that he and his fellow campmates needed the encouragement, so he wrote out as much Scripture as he could remember.

Every time I think of this incident, I am reminded of how important it is for us to read and meditate on Scripture. **When we get God's words inside of our hearts, they will return to our minds when we need them most.** My uncle counseled many victims and soldiers who gave their lives to Christ and vowed to live for Him. Soldiers who were once so cold and ruthless experienced a complete change of heart.

My uncle survived that horrid time and was released, thanks to the Russian workers from the flourmill who intervened for him, telling the officers how good he was to them during their time together. This taught me an important lesson regarding business, and it's this: **be kind to the people you manage and treat them with respect. You never know what position they may hold in your life one day.**

Thankfully, my uncle returned to his family safely, positively affecting hundreds of people along the way. In the midst of the clouds, he had found his silver lining. Sure, he could've played the victim card, staying stuck in his misery. But instead, he chose to make the most of his position, to turn his negative into a positive. Because he did, many gave their hearts to God and were given a second chance, an opportunity to spend eternity with Christ.

For a Season, For a Reason

One day, after I had already moved to Canada, my mother got into a bad bicycle accident. A car ran into her at full speed, causing her to break several ribs, puncture her head, and cut up her legs terribly. The driver of the car fractured her skull, but thankfully, both lived.

Even though she insisted that she was fine, Dad had a nurse move into the house to care for Mother while he was away at work. Sigi and Christel were the only ones still living at home at the time, and Sigi was not a fan of this woman. She thought she was too strict, and she didn't want her around. The nurse could feel Sigi's resistance, so she slowly began to reach out to her. She started to spend her off time with her, teaching her what she knew about caring for others and sharing her heart about why her job was important.

This woman inspired Sigi to become a nurse. The terrible accident that Mother had brought an enormous blessing into Sigi's life and helped her make her next big decision. **Things often happen for a season and for a reason. That's why we should never give up, always looking at the *why* behind the *what* of every circumstance we encounter.**

That's what I've learned to do. Now, when I'm faced with a tough situation, I immediately begin looking for the silver lining. I ask myself, *What good can come from this?* God always works for the good of those who love Him, and who stay called according to His purpose.[8]

The Transfer

As I mentioned before, after my divorce from Judy, I was completely heartbroken. I felt that all I had ever known and loved had come to an abrupt end, and there was nothing I could do about it, as badly as I wanted to do something.

Along with losing my wife, I also felt that I had lost my purpose. That feeling brought a deeper sorrow into my life than I thought was possible. The hurt my heart felt was beyond anything I thought I could bear. It seemed that even if I worked incredibly hard for the rest of my life, I would never fulfill all the plans God had for me. I had already messed it up, and it could not be recovered.

What a refreshing moment it was when I realized that is not how God works. He is a merciful God; He is always ready to pick us up and set us back on our feet. I was not doomed to failure just because I had fallen. He still had plans to give me an incredible hope and a future.

As I rested in God's peace and watched Him work in my life and in the lives of those around me, I soon found that my purpose wasn't gone; it was just transferred. I was given a new avenue to fulfill it through my charity

---

[8] Romans 8:28

work, and my sister was given the parts of it that I felt I couldn't handle.

God will always find a way to get his purpose accomplished, even when we fail. Even when we make mistakes, He'll never leave us out. I genuinely believe that the dream I left behind, the dream that I loved so deeply was transferred to a person that I loved deeply so that I could still have part in it. It was given to my sister, Sigi.

Sigi grew up in the same household I did, learning about the same God I did. But while she was in nursing school, the strong influence of communism in the curriculum began to weigh on her. In her class, all the religious instruction had been stopped. The children were openly taught not to attend church anymore, and as a result, most became indifferent to the teachings of the Bible. It wasn't long before nearly every person in Sigi's class had joined the Communist Party, and because she didn't want to be left out, so did little Sigi, as well as Christel.

Back then, if you weren't a part of the party, you couldn't play sports or join in school activities. As you got older, you couldn't even attend high school or college because they didn't want to raise "enemies of the state." Even in the classroom, you were outright mistreated. You could have technically earned 100 percent on a test, but the highest grade they would give you was 80 or 85 percent. You just couldn't win in their system!

> ### In Their Words
>
> *In the Communist system, America was our enemy. We learned that they were the ones who were against us, but in my heart, I wasn't so sure. When I was a toddler, we would get care packages from America with cheese, milk, tea, butter, clothes, and a lot of necessities. I told my mother that I just knew the teachers were lying! There was no way America could be our enemy because they were trying to help us. Even as a young child, America touched my heart, and that never changed, despite what anyone else said. (Christel Preik, sister)*

There were certainly advantages of joining the Communist Movement, but there were some disadvantages as well. You had to go on long, grueling marches instead of playing at recess; you had to attend brainwashing-type sessions, and you were constantly encouraged to separate from your parents. They would even encourage the children to tattle on their parents if they did things the government did not agree with—things as simple as listening to "the voice of America" on the American radio stations.

Many kids were so brainwashed that they actually turned their parents in, and as a result, they were taken from the parents and retrained in the ways of communism. It was a tumultuous time, and it affected Sigi greatly. What she learned during that season of her life completely changed her for the worse.

On my visit home to introduce Judy to the family and to continue my Bible studies, I found that the Sigi I had left in Berlin was not the Sigi that had visited me in Canada, nor was it the Sigi I came home to. Although she knew God was real, she wanted nothing to do with the church.

In Germany at that time, the church was extremely strict, stricter than it should have been. The Gospel was made unattractive. You couldn't even tap your feet to music without being scolded. The freedom that comes with living the Christian life had gotten lost in the manmade laws of religion.

One day, I was sitting in the living room visiting with my father when Sigi burst into the room. She had been gone for several months and was still supposed to be in Sweden, where she had been for the last several months living with her Swedish friend. To our surprise, she waltzed in looking like a totally different girl than the one we had known.

I'm sure our faces looked shocked as she stood in front of us, with a bit too much makeup on and a dress that was a few inches too short. Dad was livid. His face turned bright red, and he let her have it. When I saw that their argument was getting them nowhere, I intervened and tried to settle the situation.

After everyone calmed down, I comforted my father by assuring him that I would talk to Sigi. We talked about everything. She opened up to me, informing me just why she wanted nothing to do with the faith we had grown up to cherish. She said that she wanted to have an exciting life, and she thought there was no way to do that as a Christian. In her heart, she started to wonder if God was even real; and if He was, how He could let bad things happen to innocent people.

I could see my little sister's faith fading, and it was breaking my heart. I prayed that somehow God would show me what to say. I knew how it felt to wonder if you had missed out on your purpose, and I certainly did not want her walking down that road.

I really believe God gave me the words to say that day. I challenged Sigi's way of thinking, ensuring her of God's plans for her to have an exciting life with Him. I'm not sure what it was that connected with her, but I do remember the moment that I saw a change in her eyes. It was as if, in one moment, her heart was softened to the things of God once again. Her voice shook as she asked if we could rededicate her life to God right then and there.

Both of our eyes were teary as we kneeled down and prayed. When she got up, she seemed like a completely different person. She seemed just as passionate about loving the church as she had been about hating it only hours before. It wasn't long before she too had enrolled in a Bible school and began diving deeply into learning about Christ.

In Their Words

I'll never forget when Rein came back to Germany. He said he felt that God wanted to do something in our family. I remember seeing him kneel in our living room as he prayed for us. He was the instrument that God used to stimulate me, to break me open, and to help me do just what the Lord wanted me to do. It seemed as if he would've given up everything just to make me believe. (Sigi Oblander, sister)

Today, Sigi is an amazing preacher. She and her husband David still travel six to seven months out of the year, bringing the Good News of Jesus to people all around the world. Hundreds of thousands of people have been impacted by their ministry.

I believe that God knew the trouble I would have in my marriage to Judy in the months that followed and that I wouldn't be in the position to pursue ministry full-time like I had wanted. He was already making preparations to make the best out of my situation. My sister became the evangelist, and I supported her. She went, and I sent.

This all seems so clear now, but it wasn't all that clear before. I am just thankful that **God doesn't waste anything. He will take our mistakes and use them for His glory**. He will turn our desperate situations into hope-filled ones.

I sit back often and think to myself, *How did I end up here? How is it possible to have such a great life, when there were so many things that tried to hold me back?* The bombings in East Germany, life under Hitler's dictatorship, poverty, failed marriages, injuries, illnesses, deaths of loved ones, and the list goes on.

Now, I know why. It's because I stayed focused on the good, even when everything seemed bad. I remained thankful for every season, never regretting one of them but allowing them to lead me right where I was supposed to be.

6

How to Be Thankful for Every Season

Never Regret a Step

"*How* long will it take to build this thing?" I remembered asking Jerry Lackey, the founder of Love Botswana, the organization we are working with.

"Oh, it will take at least fourteen months. It's a process," he said. "You've got to mix the concrete, lay it, wait for that to dry, cut the steel, and then raise it up. And that's just the frame."

"That long?" I asked, thinking through the building process again. I was ready to get this building built and open to the sweet people of Botswana.

"Yes, but that's the only way it'll last around here. A good, solid building just takes time."

"A good, solid building does take time," I thought to myself. Just like anything. Nothing solid can ever be built on a weak foundation, and that includes our lives. That's why we should be thankful for every step in the process, every season in our progress, no matter how long or how hard it seems.

Live for any significant amount of time, and you'll find that life is growth. You don't just start at the top.

You go through experiences, one on top of another, each one preparing you a little more for the coming season. You take one small step after the next, until eventually, you open your eyes to find you're exactly where you should be.

Only then can you look back and realize how God had his hand on you the whole time. Only then will you find that it wasn't just one event or one person that brought your success. It was the whole string of people and places and happenings that brought you to where you are. Until then, it's vital to learn to be thankful for every season, present, and past.

I learned this truth during the worst part of the war. Food was so scarce that we could hardly keep enough around to survive. I hated those times, yet I learned to be grateful in the midst of them for anything that we did have and grateful out of them for all that I had learned.

Around 1946, two events occurred that caused my family, along with the entire country, to suffer greatly: inflation and the reduction of food stamps. By this time, the Reich mark (the German currency at the time) had been drastically devaluated, as it was totally dependent on the black market, the trading of goods illegally. Everything was now five to ten times the usual price. It became so devalued that bread, which was our staple food, was unaffordable to the majority of the population.

If you could find stores that had managed to stay open, it was nearly impossible to find food on the shelves. Because of the heavy bombing, the bridges and railways were destroyed, and there was no way for farmers to bring produce to citizens. Millions of people were on the verge of starving to death. We had even heard rumors of people eating human flesh to keep themselves alive.

Then one Monday morning, we all woke up to learn that the food stamps we had been using for several months had also been devalued. With food stamps, each family member got a certain amount according to their age that could be traded for so many grams of fat, starch, and protein. Because of this reduction, we got less food per stamp, which hit most families hard. These little pieces of paper with tear-off edges were the most prized possession in every household, even more important to us than money. They were our only hope of survival. Now, we weren't sure even they could keep us fed.

Mother went to the store often to try to make the most of our rationing tickets. Meat and dairy products were hard to come by. One egg per person per week was a normal ration, and if we were lucky we got Berlin "coffee," which was actually crushed acorn. We got excited when we were able to purchase a bit of the artificial margarine that had been chemically fabricated.

Mom would sometimes send Sigi and Christel (who were barely preteens at the time) to smuggle cheese and chocolates home from West Berlin. We tried our hardest to preserve the food, but we would often go through what should be a month's worth in only a week. One night, I barely recognized Dad when he walked in. His body had gotten so much more slim and frail than the stout, strong man I was used to seeing.

I'd never experienced hunger like this before. This kind of hunger was painful, almost crippling. There were many times I almost vomited out of starvation, but there was nothing inside to come out. Our stomachs shrunk so that we got to the point that we didn't even expect food; we just ate it every so often to keep ourselves going, and we learned to be happy with that. We found truth in the prayer, "Give us this day our daily bread" because day-to-day is how we lived.

By this time, Dad was still at his job, working hard to make what money he could. Mom became a "rubble lady," as did many of our friends and neighbors. Rubble ladies were women who scoured the city picking up the leftover bricks from the debris after an explosion. They then piled up all the old bricks, and from there they tried to rebuild using the same materials. They didn't get paid much, but it was something, and anything helped.

We kids worked hard to assist Mother in making the most of what we had. We saved up the little money that we had from trading to purchase chickens, goats, and rabbits to provide eggs, milk, cream, and some meat. We also kept up Opa's vegetable garden, which became our salvation in such hard times.

My favorite dinners were ones in which we had fresh potatoes or beets from the garden. We also made it a habit of going out into the forest to look for mushrooms. We typically came back with sacks full and then spent hours at the table separating the poisonous ones from the good ones.

Sometimes, when we were really desperate for food, we searched for a certain type of nettle that didn't sting, and Mom would cook that. For snacks, we picked dandelions and ate them. When we had nothing else, at least Mom could make cabbage soup or beet and corncob mush to last us for the last couple of days until we got new ration tickets. For treats, if we had leftover wheat buns to spare, Mother gave them to us. We poked holes in the middle of them and filled them with sugar. Those were our favorite desserts.

After a couple of months, Dad decided he'd had enough of watching his family starve. We kids were suffering from malnutrition, and it was becoming obvious. He quit his job at the gas company, since they weren't paying him much anyway, and focused solely on procuring food for his family. After all, what good was a little bit of money when there was no food to be bought? And even if there were food to be bought, how much good would that little bit really do?

Because the money had become so devalued that it could hardly buy us anything, Dad traded valuables for food. He put his artistic abilities to use and traded his beautiful paintings. Everyone loved Dad's work, so there was always a demand for it. We usually got about twenty loaves of bread for each painting which, to us, felt like striking a gold mine.

Once Dad sold a painting to a dentist and got money instead. It was a whole suitcase of money and still only bought ten loaves of bread.

After the war, Dad returned to his career as a tool and dye maker; but before that, he initiated several business ventures. He would literally do anything to keep our family alive and healthy. First, he started a business making concrete shingles with the steel molds we used for the rooftop of our bunker. Opa had an old machine Dad refurbished to do the work of making the shingles on.

This business only lasted for about a year because under the postwar Communist system, it was nearly impossible to get decent amounts of cement. Next, he teamed up with his brother Helmut to make leather harnesses for horses. People in the country didn't have the gas to go to town, so they used horses for transport. Dad would take a train out there and go farm to farm, trading the harnesses for food.

Dad traded many things, but the day Mom tearfully offered to sell her wedding ring was the day we knew we'd hit rock bottom. She had already given up all her jewelry, fine china, and many other valuable items, but still we needed more. We only got a few loaves of bread for the ring, which made the situation even more disheartening.

I was about twelve years old at this time, and I wanted to contribute to my family. So I begged and begged to go along on my dad's weekly excursions. It took a while, but he finally agreed. I started skipping school regularly on the premise that at this point, food was more important than education. We rode on tops of trains tying ourselves to the air ducts and lying down flat so that we would be safe going through tunnels. It was extremely dangerous, but we knew we didn't have much of a choice.

Some trips were two or three days long. Those trips were some of the most frustrating yet rewarding experiences I had ever had. Sometimes, we got a good deal; other times we didn't. I hated coming back with just a loaf of bread or a couple of pounds of potatoes. But when we struck a big deal, it felt like a party in the Preik house!

Many times on the road, we begged for sandwiches from farmers. Most people were nice enough to give us a piece of bread and butter to split or a bowl of soup for each of us. On these excursions, we often walked about ten miles with twenty to thirty pounds of potatoes on our backs, and we'd think nothing of it. We were just that happy to have food! And so was everyone else. There was always an eruption of applause as soon as we walked through the door.

"Oh, yay! Rein and Daddy are home!" I heard the girls squeal. Everyone dropped what they were doing the moment we stepped inside.

"Show us what you got this time!" Their little faces beamed with excitement. Dad and I would then reveal our findings, and although it would not be much, the girls and Mother would praise us for it. They were so thankful. We all were.

The worst days were the days that Dad and I returned with nothing. I'll never forget the sight of the little girls holding back tears as we walked in empty-handed. Mom looked discouraged as she went out to the garden and picked a utica plant, a stinging nettle, and cooked it. It was sad to watch this caring mother and amazing cook feel that she could not prepare a satisfying meal for her family.

We knew we weren't the only ones facing this, so we tried to stay positive, but it was hard. Many people were depressed, and we heard often about neighbors and distant acquaintances ending their lives to get rid of the pain. I have to admit that although I didn't approve of their choice, I completely understood the pain that led them to make it.

It was a tough time for all of us, and things got even tougher once winter hit. The coal ration was insufficient—only twenty-five kilograms per family for the entire winter. We needed wood for a fire so that we could heat the house. At first, Mother and Dad cut down birch trees illegally and loaded them onto a cart hidden under other things. People who did this were often fined heavily or even sent to prison. I fully expected for my parents to not come home one day, but thankfully, they never got caught.

They repeated this trip nearly every week, as did many other families, so it wasn't very long before all the trees were gone. That's why today in Berlin, nearly all the trees are the same age. Everything had to be replanted after the war.

I went with my Dad the few times that Mom couldn't. When we arrived in the forest, I was surprised to see that there were only stumps left. We had to dig them up, which was harder than chopping a tree. It was freezing, and we hardly had any clothes. We had to walk several miles just to get there, and we were typically there for the entire day.

One day, I was out digging stumps when the ax slipped and cut a gash in between my toes, on the only boots I had. Today, that doesn't seem like a big deal; but back then, it was because I wasn't sure when I would receive another pair of shoes. A knot appeared in my stomach as soon as it happened. What was I going to tell Mother? How long would it be before we could repair them?

Life as we knew it had drastically changed. What was once a necessity had now become a luxury. There was no private transportation, no paint, no cosmetics, no glass to fix windows, no buying clothes, and hardly any shoes at all. At one point, we were only allowed electricity once a day, between 11:00 p.m. and 1:00 a.m. We learned to live with the bare minimum.

Some of the necessities we received from organizations in West Berlin through donations made by Americans. There we picked up valuables such as winter coats, Sunday dresses, children's clothes, cheese, and milk powder. It was dangerous to accept these things because of the risk of carrying them back to East Berlin, but we did so out of desperation. And again, we didn't get caught.

No matter how bad things were, I will never look back on those rough times with resentment or bitterness because I know that they brought me to the place of gratefulness that I live in every single day. Never will I take my blessings for granted because I know how it is for them to be taken away in a moment.

The startling truth is that it can happen to anyone. One day you're living good, and then all of a sudden, something of incredible worth is stripped from you. Whether it's money, possessions, or even a loved one, it's in those times that you truly learn to be grateful—grateful for what you have and grateful for those who stand by you.

Mother and Dad after the war, 1950

Not About the Physical

When you endure a season like this, your whole idea of what is valuable changes. Never before had I thought that money could actually become worthless, but it did. Right after the war, the German bank had to get control of the money going out, so they took some German Reich marks and put stamps on it, sort of like postage stamps. The stamped money was the only money that could be used for a while, until the West and East decided to start printing their own money. Because most of the goods to buy were in the West, most of the East Berliners crossed over to shop. They exchanged their money at booths set up in West Berlin at the border.

The problem with this was that the exchange rate was typically four East DMs for one West DM, making normal life nearly impossible for any East Berliners. All of a sudden, those who were extremely wealthy became like everyone else. Now, it didn't matter how much you had; everything got evened out. Those working in the East got poorer, and those working in the West got more affluent.

Those were some of the hardest times, but they gave me the biggest wake-up call. I learned quickly that the physical is not all there is. You can have money today and not tomorrow. You can have cars today and not tomorrow. Those things will fade fast, but if you keep your faith and have positive, loving, and supportive people around you, you have everything you need to build a life worth living.

Not long ago, I mentioned to Jennifer that I might want to sell one of our houses in North Carolina. Her sentimental side kicked in, and she teared up as she tried to discourage me with all the beautiful memories we had made together in that house.

"How are you so detached?" she asked.

How could I not be? I thought.

Growing up, moving from place to place, I had to detach myself from everything because it could be there one day and gone the next. The fact is that you might have an empty stomach, but if you have a house full of people who love you, you have something to be thankful for. You might feel discouraged, but **if you have faith and determination to see a better tomorrow, you have all that you need to turn your life around.**

A Final Good-bye

By the late 1950s, I started to grow more and more concerned for my family. I knew that communism had gotten worse as well as the economic situation in Berlin. Being in Canada while most of them were still stuck living in the terrible conditions in East Germany was rough for me. So many times I encouraged them to move over, but Dad never wanted to leave.

At first, he didn't want to leave because Opa was so old and ill that he couldn't travel. After Opa passed away, he didn't want to leave the house they had worked so hard to build together. He also knew that he could get a job in Germany, but he was not so sure about his chances in Canada, although I tried to convince him otherwise.

Several times, I sent them letters instructing them to cross the border from East to West Berlin on the given date, at the given time. I sent them an address of a house to go to in West Berlin. I knew a family who had a telephone that they would allow them to use. It would take them an hour to get to the house, and then they would wait for an hour to two for me to call. It was nearly a day-long trip for them just to hear my voice for a few minutes.

Each time I talked to them, it was brief, but my message was clear: They needed to get out of Berlin. I watched the news closely and knew that there was going to be some kind of drastic measure taken. I was right; not long after one of my warnings, the Berlin Wall was built. That caused a slew of problems, especially for those living in the east. By that point, the homeless wanted to stay and take advantage of the system, but the professionals just wanted out because as it was said in East Berlin, "Life is better on the other side of the wall." There, you didn't have to suffer from the throes of communism.

Like most people, Mom desperately wanted to leave East Berlin, but Dad didn't. I guess it's true that the man is the head of the home, but the woman is the neck that turns the head because Dad eventually agreed to leave. He made the decision after an incident threatened our family's privacy and possibly their safety.

One day, a police officer came to the door to tell Mother that they would be forced to take people without a home into their own. Dad was afraid they were going to place a Communist spy in their home to make sure that they didn't escape. Their time was running out.

About this time, Mother had the bad accident. She invited the nurse to stay with them so that they could fill a spot in the house until they could find a way to leave quietly. We all knew it wasn't going to be easy for them to get out. By that time, everyone was watching each other's homes. You couldn't even trust your own neighbors.

The East Berlin police knew its citizens were trying to escape, so they were doing everything within their power to keep them there. In fact, they were calling my parents "enemies of the state" and following them around town.

One day, a party leader told my Mother, "You're on our black list. Your family is just the kind we don't want around here."

Oftentimes, they knocked on their door asking if they had anyone staying with them and insisting on searching their house. That was especially scary for them when Ursula, who had escaped to West Germany a couple of years earlier, went home to visit. She would fly into West Berlin and take a streetcar to my parents' house; but when the wall went up, that was no longer possible.

On one visit, the secret police heard reports from neighbors that she was home, and they became suspicious. The officers came by their house every few days, so my family would have to hide Ursula and pray that the men wouldn't find her. If they had found her, they would have made her stay, and her entire escape would have been useless.

That was a scary time for everyone. People would be scared just to talk in their own homes because they never knew when someone was right outside their door listening.

Mother finally grew sick of all the rules and came up with a plan: she, Sigi, and Christel, who were barely teenagers, would each take one suitcase at a time filled with things from the house, carry it to a friend's apartment in the West and leave it there. That way, when they got to the West, they would have some things to take with them.

To smuggle these things over the border, the girls had to trick the police. They typically went during rush hour so that they were less likely to get noticed. Sigi and Christel were so little that they could hide behind people. Oftentimes, they jumped from one train to another, trying hard to be inconspicuous, so that no one questioned them.

Once they almost had everything out of the house, something unusual happened. Although he was meeting his payments, Mom's friend was told that he couldn't keep the apartment any longer. Mom was devastated. She had spent so many days working on their escape! She, Sigi, and Christel went to work the next few weeks bringing everything back home. Although she was discouraged, that didn't stop her. It wasn't the first time she'd had to leave her things behind.

Still, Mother and Dad decided that they needed to make their move as soon as possible. So one evening,

Mom, Dad, Sigi, and Christel said good-bye to their neighborhood and left their house for West Berlin. Mom and Dad went down their street to the right, and Sigi and Christel went to the left; that way, the neighbors wouldn't notice that they were leaving for good. Once they got to the bus station, they took the same bus, pretending that they didn't know each other. Then they took a streetcar, using the same strategies the whole way there.

Once they were across the border, they flew from the West Berlin airport to West Germany. When they landed, the CIA got in touch with Dad and put him in a refugee camp for a while. They were friendly to him. They gave him a place to stay, and he provided them with information from the war. He had worked in a Russian-controlled factory, and the Americans wanted to know what they were doing in that plant.

My family lived in that camp for a few months, while I anxiously awaited some kind of message that they had been released. When I got the call that they were on their way to Canada, I was so relieved. I set the phone down, said a prayer of gratitude, and let a few tears fall from my eyes. They were all together and safe once again.

After they let my family go, my parents found a nice apartment in Hanover. It wasn't big. There were three bedrooms, one bathroom, a kitchen, and a living room. They were given a one-time allowance in lieu of losing their home in East Berlin, with which they could have either bought a house or rented an apartment. Mom chose to rent because she was tired of having to care for a house. Although I understand her reasoning, this ended up being a big mistake because they were unable to build up any kind of equity.

With Mother and Dad at their apartment in Hanover, 1962

Dad got a nice job nearby, and they got connected to a small Baptist church there. Although they had enough money, Mother also went to work. She worked in Hanover at a factory that specialized in making women's clothing. She was required to work ten years in order to get a pension, but after about nine, she stopped working because of ill health.

I went to go visit Mother and Dad as soon as I could. We all shared a good cry when I got there, as well as a prayer of thanks to God for getting them there safely. Throughout the evening, I couldn't help but stare at my parents. When did they get so old? It was obvious that the tough life they lived had taken a toll on their bodies. Dad's once thin body had become more full, and he was now showing off a round belly, which became even rounder in the years to come.

I soon found out why when Mother brought out a huge feast she had been preparing all day. I could see that she loved finally being able to feed Dad her famous meals that she was unable to prepare for him during wartime. Even after his second plate, she'd say, "Walter, there's still some in the pot," and he would go finish it off. It's a lot harder to waste food when you have lived in scarcity for so long.

With Dad, 1965

Ursula, Christel, Mother, and Sigi, 1999

There Are No Shortcuts

In racing, I've learned that no matter how much I want there to be, there are no shortcuts. When a shortcut is attempted in a race, you're typically disqualified.

The same is true in life. Sure, if we were perfect and if life was perfect, there would be no obstacles. But we're not, and neither is life, so sometimes we have to take the long way around. In those times, we have to remember that the long way is okay. It's not the end of the world if we make mistakes because it's never too late to get where we need to be. **Wherever our "there" is, we can always get there from where we are.**

The fact is that **those things we want to regret are the things that have made us into who we are today.** I was twenty-three years old when I got married the first time. I hadn't dated anyone. I was lonely, so I was quick to jump on board without even taking the time to learn as much as I should've about my new bride. Perhaps I married too soon, or perhaps I married the wrong person. Whatever the case, I learned from that situation that when making important decisions, I should be more thorough.

The second time, I again made the mistake of marrying too soon, but this time without completely going through the necessary healing process. That's what happens when you don't give your situation completely over to God. You try to make things happen on your own, and you end up off worse than you were before.

Because of my immaturity, I made a few bad decisions, and I suffered for it. The weight of the condemnation that I felt for having been through two divorces was almost unbearable because when I was growing up, divorce wasn't as accepted as it is today. It was looked down upon as one of the worst choices you could make, especially if you were a follower of Christ.

I struggled with this guilt on a daily basis, until one day I was given advice that completely changed my perspective. I heard that I could either look back on my failed relationships, continuing to regret those mistakes that I had made, or I could choose to be thankful for that season in my life, for how it made me a better husband to Jennifer and a better father to our children. I chose the latter, and I'm so glad I did.

Today, Jennifer's daughter Erin is now my daughter, and my children—Marc, Krista, Quentin, Austin, and Curtis—have become her own. Now I'll never regret a step, because I know that God is always working for the good in my life and in the lives of those around me. He always uses the lessons we have learned to better the rest of our lives. In order to receive them though, we must accept the fact that there are no shortcuts in life.

We've got to learn from our mistakes, not regret them. As we take it one step at a time, we'll eventually open our eyes to find that we're right where we're meant to be.

Seasons

Obviously, we don't go from mistake to strength right away. It's like building muscle. It has to be broken down before it can be built back up. We have to break down first, experience a little bit of the pain and heal properly before God can use our experiences to make us stronger. Sometimes these times are needed just so that we can be sure of the reality of God.

Faith comes in seasons too. It starts growing even when we don't see it. The fall comes, then the winter, and *then* the spring. You have times when it seems dry. Nothing seems to be growing. But it is. You've just got to be patient.

If we knew everything from the start, we probably wouldn't make the decisions we were meant to make.

For instance, I probably wouldn't have taken a couple of years to attend Bible School or pastor churches if I had known that my career was going to take me the business route. But God knew what was up ahead.

He knew that I would be working closely with churches, pastors, missionaries, and church leaders. He knew that I would need to know how that world worked. Now, I have a better understanding of the people and requirements involved because of those seemingly pointless years of ministry training.

That's why we've got to trust, even when we don't understand. **The place you're in now is the perfect preparation for a future that only God can see. You don't know what's up ahead, but you don't have to. You don't have to be certain of the road ahead, as long as you're certain of the One leading you.**

The fact is that you can plan as much as you want, but life always seems to take you in a different direction. In the times it looks like it's impossible to make it through, when we wonder why God would even allow such a problem in our life, we have to stand strong. We should never fight or resist; instead, we should accept the growth and the change. It's like sandpaper. It's uncomfortable at first, but the more we rub against it, the smoother and more polished we become.

Looking Back

A few years after we were married, Jennifer and I went back to my former home in East Berlin. It was an emotional experience, to say the least. The house was in reasonable shape, although it was much smaller than I remembered. Seeing it made me thankful—not thankful for the terrible time we had, necessarily, but thankful for the man it made me, for the foundation it built in my life.

Sigi and Christel in front of our house in East Berlin, 2010

In Germany, under Hitler, we had nothing. We felt that we *were* nothing, but through God's grace, we have made our lives into something—something beautiful to be used for His glory. Today, I live with purpose because I know that **God never wastes a hurt.** He never regrets a step in our lives, so why should we? We might just be able to see the few steps in front of us, but He can see the entire road ahead. We see today, but he sees a lifetime.

When you're young, it's hard to understand your purpose in all its fullness. But as you near the end of God's path for your life, it all becomes clearer.

Over eighty years ago, before I was even a thought in my parents' minds, God knew the purposes He was creating me for. Like the Bible says, God knew me before I was formed in my mother's womb. Before I was born, He had set me apart.[9] And He has done the same for you.

---

[9] Jeremiah 1:5

7
How Generosity Brings Joy

Hands and Feet

---·◆·---

*T*he ceremony is just about to start. From a distance, I see my two sons, Quentin and Curtis, who have also come to celebrate with us. I look down the row and see the minister of justice and the minister of defense for Botswana. The president was scheduled to speak, but I found out just as we were walking in that he had to cancel last minute. I can already see that it is going to be a festive program, with singing, dancing, and colorful banners waving through the air.

The ceremony is being held as a celebration for both the Lackey's twenty-five years of service in Botswana as well as for the opening of the center. I try hard to hide the few tears finding their way down my face, but there is no stopping them. Jennifer reaches over to squeeze my hand as if to say, "It's all right." Just thinking of how far my life has come—from that little German boy with only a desire to do something great, to a seventy-seven-year-old man with the privilege to bless so many people. I feel so honored that God chose to use me for such a beautiful task.

As everyone gathers into the new forty-thousand-square-foot building, Jerry and Jana call Jennifer and me forward. Jennifer looks at me as if to say, "Do you think you can do it?" I nod, and we walk up with the rest of the group. Jerry and a few of the nation's *prominent leaders speak to the adult guests and children through a translator. Every few seconds, an excited yell or handclap slips out of one of them.*

"This center's mandate is to provide programs that will address the spiritual and moral growth of our youth in this community and in this nation to help to encourage entrepreneurial skills among them," Jerry explains.

"I thank all of you for being a part of starting the change in these young people's lives."

Applause erupts. This really will change their lives, I think to myself. And the kids know it. You can see it on their faces, and just seeing those looks makes every dime spent worth it. It makes every struggle in the process seem incredibly insignificant.

Next, the minister of justice speaks. "Ladies and gentlemen: Love Botswana Outreach Mission . . . is an essential ingredient in our effort to assist young people in the work intervention . . . to address social ills plaguing our communities. It is my ardent hope and prayer that the facilities placed on these premises would be effective interventions in our society and that our government can join hands with this foundation to help our young people."

Again, applause erupts. Everyone is so excited. When it comes my turn to say a few words, I am a bit nervous. I manage to get myself together so that I can address the people.

"I'm so blessed seeing this project completed," I begin.

"It's a special one because it's not just the end of a project. It's the beginning of a purpose, your purpose. You're being blessed so that you can be a blessing to others. God wants you to be His hands and feet to carry His love to those that need it most. And now, I can tell you that there's nothing greater."

With that, the ceremony ends, the ribbon is cut, and the people flood throughout the building. One by one, they come up to me, wrapping their arms around me and thanking me for my contribution. Little do they know that this project probably means just as much to me as it does to them. Maybe more.

When we sold Chemcraft, we knew our work was not yet done, that God had blessed us above and beyond for a reason—to help others. So we took a portion of the sales and established a 501c3, a nonprofit organization. Our board consists of myself, Jennifer, Diana Hyunen, the CFO of my former company, and all our children who reside in the United States (because as a rule for U.S. organizations, all board members must be located in the United States.) Two of my favorite days of the year are board meeting days, where we come together to pray and decide what projects to take on that year.

> ### In Their Words
>
> *The foundation is such a help to Christian ministries. Unlike a lot of organizations, each project is thoroughly planned out and prayed about. We don't want to be just giving a hundred dollars here, a thousand dollars there, and ten thousand there. We don't just throw money around; we are more focused with it. The Preik Family Foundation is focused on starting and finishing projects. (Austin Preik, son)*

Originally, we had decided that we didn't want to work with any bricks and mortars. We only wanted to work with individuals, one person at a time. But in our final analysis, it became very plain to us that God had specific groups He wanted us to work with. We had a tough time deciding what the first project would be. Instead of jumping right into discovering it, we decided to celebrate our retirement with a trip to Africa with some of our closest friends.

Finding Love Botswana

Botswana was our first stop on the trip. On the way there, a man took the open seat next to Jennifer on the plane. He was a vibrant young man with no accent. Jennifer loves conversation, so naturally the two struck one up right away. He introduced himself as a Methodist minister on his way back to Botswana to continue his work there. As the dialogue progressed, it became more obvious that this man had a heart for Botswana, specifically for those suffering from HIV.

He gave Jennifer startling statistic after statistic regarding the amount of people with HIV in his region. The northern part of the country, which is full of wildlife, so pristine and untouched by civilization, is the hardest hit by the pandemic. This results in a lost generation of parents and a rising number of orphans. It wasn't long before Jennifer was also close to tears.

As we touched ground in Botswana, we said good-bye to our new friend. We parted ways, but

Jennifer didn't forget the encounter we'd had. After a wonderful stay in Botswana, Pretoria, and finally, Capetown, we got ready to return home. Jennifer could not get the man and his words out of her mind. On the plane ride home, his words resurfaced in conversation. After hearing the statistics, it started to wear on me too.

We talked about what we could do and before long had decided that this was to be part of our newfound mission. Our careers might have come to an end, but this was the beginning of something new, something risky but so incredibly fulfilling. I suggested that we begin our efforts by helping this Methodist minister that we couldn't seem to forget.

Immediately, Jennifer started calling around, searching for him. She called everyone she could think of but had no luck. Even the Methodist diocese was in the dark, saying that they hadn't even placed a minister in Botswana. We were confused at first, but the bewilderment wore off as we considered the thought that perhaps this man was used especially by God to lead us into the next phase of our destiny.

We prayed about the encounter and felt in our hearts that we should still pursue work in Botswana. However, we were confident that we were not to relocate to the region ourselves, as we still had family and affairs to care for in the states. Instead, we would partner with someone who was already known throughout Botswana and was making a tangible difference in the area. We began the search for a partner right away.

In every Internet search we conducted, there was one organization at the top of the list: Love Botswana. We had no idea what this organization was, but we scrolled and clicked around until we found out more. The organization was founded by Jerry and Jana Lackey, an American couple with a passion for reaching those who had never heard nor felt the love of Christ.

Through a variety of methods, they develop these once down-and-out young people into world-changing leaders. Their Web site alone was enough to convince me that this couple could be the answer to our prayer. The next morning, Jennifer called and spoke with them briefly about their work. It took no time to decide that they were the ones we wanted to partner with. We told them we would like to help financially on any project that still needed finished.

They sounded rather shocked but excitedly filled us in on the details of a preschool building that had been put on hold. They gave us the amount, and we sent them the check. As the building was being built, so was our relationship with the Lackeys. After that project was completed, we were prepared to offer our help on another. That's when we knew God was involved in this relationship.

In Jennifer's next conversation with Jana, she informed her that she was flying to the states soon and that she would love to meet with us. She was coming to spend some time with her father in his last days and to get her son settled in for college. We were in the same area visiting our daughter Erin, so we met up with Jana at Disneyworld in Orlando. We met her kids briefly and then had breakfast with Jana at a nearby hotel.

God's timing is always perfect. We have grown to become great friends and partners with the Lackeys and Love Botswana, and since then, we've completed several other projects with them. When we hear about a need there, we do our best to meet it.

Once, we heard about a series of break-ins that had occurred on one of the Love Botswana campuses that lodged the school, housing, and several other projects in the works. Out of concern for their security, we were able to meet their long-standing need to erect a security fence on the property with a proper gatehouse to monitor all traffic in and out of the acreage.

This came at the perfect time because the next project was one that required top security. It was the building of the Loratologogo Rescue Center for Babies (meaning "place of great love") which can house and care for up to seventy-six orphaned babies ages zero to three. Without this center, there would be no facility in the country to care for these babies. It also addresses the issue of child abuse, neglect, and abandonment. As a father, I become overwhelmed with emotion when I think about helpless babies now having a place to grow up safely. I am so grateful that Jennifer and I, along with the Preik Family Foundation, can have part in this.

Loratologogo Rescue Center for Babies, 2012

In Their Words

Rein and Jennifer asked us to share other Love Botswana Projects with them to look at where they might want to do more. When they did, I thought to myself, "Do more?" They already helped so much by sending that gift for the preschool. Still, I typed out on the page a list of our current projects, from least expensive to most expensive. At the very end was the dream of the rescue center for babies.

At that point, we had started the process for registering the center, but the lack of a permanent facility was part of the delay, although I didn't mention that part in the e-mail. So we sent the e-mail through and got one back the next day. They wanted more info on the rescue center.

Most of the projects we send to them have actual building plans, but this project didn't have any yet. Still, they were most interested in that project. I asked Jerry what we should do. We agreed that I should tell them how thankful we were for their willingness to help with the project but that we had no building plans, only a dream.

I went to bed that night and asked the Lord to give us direction. I was awakened in the morning with the thought fresh in my mind that we should pull out our building plans for a project that had been built a few years before. I sent the plans through with information that it was not the plans for the building; it was only meant to show them what the cost per square foot looked like.

Pressing send on that e-mail was tough. I feared I might never hear from the Preiks again. A few days went by, and I was sure I had blown my favor with them. It was simply too much money. Our worst fear was starting a project and not being able to finish it. Abandoned building projects are all over this village of Maun, and we didn't want to be one of them.

A few days later, I got a call. On the other end of the phone was Rein Preik. He slowly started to explain to me how he and Jennifer had read all the information we had sent. He told me his story about how he had left East Germany and made a wonderful life for himself in Canada and the United States. He shared about his desire to see the Gospel change lives.

At the end of the conversation, he told me, "We believe in what you and Jerry are doing there, and we want to build the rescue center for the babies." When we got off the phone, I was in utter shock. I screamed, and I cried all day long. That was only the second conversation I had with Rein Preik. To this day, each and every time I speak with him, I leave in awe of his wisdom, strong but spoken with the love of the Father. (Jana Lackey, Love Botswana)

Shortly after we finished the baby house, I overheard Jerry telling Jana that a man from Texas had pulled out of a project they had been working on. Jana's face looked distraught.

"What was the project?" I asked.

"It was what we were going to call our Life Center," she explained.

I learned that the Lackeys had another dream in their hearts for many years. It was to build a large facility that would be a place to serve the community, especially the youth of the region, many of whom suffer from HIV. After years of hosting over twenty programs targeting youth and children, they needed a building to give these programs a permanent home. They would also use this place for church services and community events.

Once I visited, I understood just why they needed this building. As I watched the community worship in a half-standing tent, I too felt they needed some grounding. I asked them how much money it would require, and we talked through the cost. It was a good deal of money, but we felt we should at least pray about it.

After a few weeks and much prayer, Jennifer and I both felt this was a project for us to take on. We went to our foundation board and presented the project to them. Everyone was for it.

After we agreed, the process moved quickly. Love Botswana signed a ninety-nine-year lease for the property, and then Jerry and I flew to Gaborone to interview architects to take on the job. Our search brought us to a man from South Africa who presented a plan, with the material list using supplies all made in Africa. Our goal was for the building to look African, not American. We liked the look of his idea, so after a few small changes, he drew up plans and returned with an estimate. The project exceeded several million dollars, which would make it the biggest project the foundation had taken on up to that point. However, I knew they needed it, so I didn't want to back down. We would trust God to go ahead of us and make the process smooth.

We signed the contract, and the construction was begun. A surveyor and an architect were hired. We ordered a cedar house to be built for my son Austin, his wife Ann Marie, and their two kids, Luke and Savannah, to live in for two years so that the project could be overseen. We didn't want to be in charge of the project; we just wanted our foundation to be closely involved with the people there so that they knew we *really* cared. We weren't just sending money.

Besides that, I didn't want Jerry to be burdened with the load of watching over the building of the center in addition to overseeing his ministry. It was also a good opportunity for Austin, who had just graduated from seminary, to gain some practical experience in mission work. The house was built on the compound so that after the project was completed, they could continue using the house for guests.

This beautiful Life Center is now finished and is home to the Village Church as well as multiple outreach programs. It is a valuable resource for the community.

We were so grateful to be a part of something that would make such a strong, practical impact both on the present and on the future of a nation.

I often think about what would have happened if, while we were searching for "the next step," I had tried to take matters into my own hands. I am certain that I could not have found better people or a better organization to partner with. Every day, I am grateful for a God to whom I can entrust with the big decisions of my life. Time and time again, He has led me to the people, projects, and ultimately the purpose that I was destined to be a part of.

The Life Center, 2012

The first service held in the Village Church, located in the Life Center, 2012

In Their Words

My father has always been consistent. I think in the back of his mind he has always been a missionary. Who he is hasn't changed. Now, he just has the opportunity to fulfill who he has always been. That's what he always wanted to do; he has just gone back to his original goal. It's not a change–it's a return. (Krista Preik, daughter)

Becoming Family

After Jennifer's wake-up call with cancer, she decided she wanted to rededicate herself to focusing on God's purpose for her life. She felt this endeavor to Africa was a new beginning for her, for us, and for our futures. She wanted to get baptized by immersion, but she didn't want to do it just anywhere. She wanted to make her profession of faith with those who had cared about her, who had prayed for her throughout that tough time.

Because Jerry had experienced stage 4 cancer just a year before that, the Lackeys understood exactly what she had faced. During that time, they, along with their congregation, joined with us in prayer every single day. That's why she wanted to be with her African family. They were the ones who had stood with her so strongly.

Jerry and I both tried to convince her to be baptized somewhere a little more comfortable, since she had recently been through cancer treatment. The Lackeys offered her a swimming pool and a private baptism, but she didn't want that. So Jerry baptized her there in the cool wintry waters one Sunday afternoon, along with several other African men, women, and children, also dedicating their lives to Christ.

That's the beautiful thing about God's family. We're all accepted. It doesn't matter who you are, what the color of your skin is, what your last name is, where you work, how talented you are, or how much money you have. We are all family.

> ### In Their Words
>
> *Jennifer has always been generous since I've known her. But I believe that the cancer scare gave her the ability to see as God sees. Just as God spit in the eye of the blind man to make him see, so he sometimes spits in our eye to make us see the world the way He does. God is using Jennifer now more than ever before. Together, Rein and Jennifer have become like a flowing river of generosity. (Sigi Oblander, sister)*

Generosity connects people in a way no other act can. It's how God included us into His family—by giving us His only Son Jesus as a sacrifice for our sins. Now we're forever connected through Him. That's the mind-set I try to live with every single day of my life. Giving someone anything—whether it's money, time, love, grace, anything at all—is one of the best things you can do for them because generosity lives on. **When you invest into someone, you then become a part of everything that they do. You are forever linked to every person they reach and every life they change.**

That thought alone thrills me. Sure, the physical gifts might fade away, but the ones we give out of a generous heart can have long-lasting effects, some even eternal.

> ## In Their Words
>
> *One day, I was eating at a restaurant in Maun when I received a startling call from Jerry. He had gone eight hours north to visit our branch church pastors. He shakily informed me that they had been in an accident. They were on edge but fine and were stranded in the remote area of Mohembo. The car was clearly totaled. It was the Jeep that we had been saving for years to get—our first brand-new car ever.*
>
> *When Rein found out, he asked me to organize for a mercy flight to go immediately to collect them and bring them home. It was a miracle that no one was hurt. From the look of the vehicle, they should have all been injured.*
>
> *A few weeks later, we got a call from Rein telling us that we needed to save room on a container that was scheduled to come over with mission supplies because he had bought a brand-new jeep for Jerry to replace the one that was totaled. These are just a few examples of the way this man's heart works. (Jana Lackey, Love Botswana)*

Prophets and Kings

We can't all give large amounts of money, but we can all give something. In the Old Testament, God shows us through the way that He uses both prophets and kings that we all have a part to play in building His church. He doesn't get His work completed with just one; He needs them working together. In story after story, the kings are the ones with the means to provide, with the resources to fund projects. The prophets are the ones out laboring in the field, seeing to it that the projects are finished.

Because of how God has blessed me, I consider myself in the king category. I have the resources to help God's work get done, but I do not oversee the day-to-day management of the projects. In my position, I've found that there is a lot of money in Christian communities; the key is to allocate our priorities to the right things.

I strongly sense that it's time for the "kings" of our day to wake up and realize our opportunity. It's time to accept responsibility, to seek out the "prophets," and to do our part to see the work completed. We are *all* needed to make a difference in the world. We are all important to the expansion of God's kingdom.

Shortly after Jennifer was diagnosed with cancer, we felt God was moving us to find a new church home. Although we loved the church we were at, we felt there was work He wanted us to do somewhere else. That's when we found Journey Church in Fernandina Beach, Florida. We had heard a lot about the good this church was doing in the community, but Jennifer was not so sure she would be welcomed among the younger, more contemporary crowd that she had heard about.

"I am not going to fit in with these people," she said. "I am too traditional!"

She thought this because Journey Church is unlike most churches. There are people of every color, denomination, and age, with clothing styles ranging from Sunday best to jeans and flip-flops. We avoided it for a few weeks, but the more good we heard and the more we saw attendance growing, the more our interest intensified. Finally, one Sunday, we decided to try it out.

We were pleasantly surprised. As we walked in, we were greeted by two sweet people and were taken to a seat in what seemed to be a rather new and casual auditorium. The music style was youthful, unlike what we were used to, but it sounded great. Then the pastor got up and delivered a positive life-giving message. His name was Darryl.

I asked Jennifer her thoughts on the way home, and sure enough, she enjoyed it. She even wanted to go back! So we did, again and again, until we decided that this was the church we would plant ourselves in. About a month later, we had the opportunity to go to lunch with Pastor Darryl and his wife, Kara. That day began a remarkable relationship that I will forever treasure.

In Their Words

The Preiks have been an anchor in our church since the moment they walked through the doors. What was intriguing is that the first time we had lunch, he didn't talk about himself, his success, or his affluence. He talked about all the things he was able to be a part of, the things he was able to pour back into the Kingdom of God. He's just not a flashy guy. He truly has a tender heart for people.

Not long after they started coming, Rein and Jennifer got involved in our food ministry, which gives out grocery items that have passed their sale date but are still fine to eat. We became a premier agency of Second Harvest, an organization out of Jacksonville, Florida, that gets those groceries and puts them in the hands of the people.

We had the opportunity to enlarge this ministry, but there were some regulations. We had to buy refrigerated trucks and expand our building. From the moment Rein heard about this opportunity to reach and feed more people, he said, "I'll do it."

The next big project we started was the building of our new sanctuary. Journey Church started in a storefront, which was an old Kmart that had moved locations. We had about eleven thousand square feet, which we outgrew in five years. We needed to find property, move and build a building. Thankfully, forty acres were donated to the church. However, because of the economy, it was hard to finance anything without some money upfront. No bank wants to put their faith in a five-year-old church!

We had to raise 1.5 million dollars for the bank to be able to loan us three million dollars. Rein told me that whatever the church brought in, he would match. We ended up raising $750,000, and he donated the other $750,000. Because of his generous gift, we were able to build a brand-new building and move to a new location.

Rein truly is a great conduit of the Kingdom of God. But that doesn't mean he always says yes. He truly prays about where he spends his money and how he spends it. He has a lot of wisdom, whether it's regarding work, life, or business. He brings so much to the table because he has been there. For him it's not about money spent; it's about people invested in.

The greatest thing that I've learned from him is that as a follower of Christ, there is no such thing as retirement. When

> *God is finished with you, you are no longer here. (Pastor Darryl Bellar, Journey Church)*

The Bellars and Journey Church have since become a large part of our lives. Since that Sunday, we have been connected to Journey Church in a way that only generosity can connect you. Darryl is a generous "prophet," studying and working hard to do the best he can with what God has given Him. We have also strived to show generosity by helping the church to impact those in our area.

The first project we took on was the building project. We greatly needed a larger auditorium due to our consistent growth. Now, our seven-hundred-fifty to eight-hundred seat sanctuary is often packed every service, even using the one-hundred-fifty-seat overflow room. Especially for a ministry that is only about seven years old, Journey Church is making a remarkable impact in our community.

External and internal views of the new Journey Church building, 2011

Next, we heard about a ministry of the church that feeds those confronted with the dangers of poverty. The demand was greater than what they could supply because the refrigeration truck was too small. We helped by buying a new one so that more people could be fed. Now, over double the amount of people are fed every week.

I don't tell you these things to draw attention to us but rather to the joys of generosity. I can honestly say that I am more fulfilled than I have ever been because I know that as I give to others, I am connecting myself to a greater vision. By touching one life, I now have a part in every other life they touch after that.

Which are you—a prophet or a king? Whichever position you are in, I hope you'll use it well. Let what is important to the heart of God become important to your heart.

> ## In Their Words
>
> *Rein is incredibly generous. Although he was frugal with the company money, he was always generous in taking care of his employees. They were always in the back of his mind. He was thoughtful about giving Christmas bonuses and making sure his staff had money for their holiday. He was adamant that the company took care of its people. Most company leaders put shareholders first, but at Chemcraft, he made sure it was customers and employees first and then shareholders second. (David Rogers, CEO of Chemcraft International)*

Give As Unto God

If you can't give money, there are plenty of other things to offer—time, expertise, love. The key is to look for what someone needs and then determine how you can fulfill that need. Years ago, when we weren't able to give as much financially, Jennifer saw a different need in a little girl named Dawn, and she decided to meet it.

She met Dawn through a mentoring program. The moment she saw her, she silently prayed this little girl would be matched with her. Dawn was a pretty, demure little sixth-grade girl; and for some reason, they just clicked. She comes from a strong Christian family with many siblings, all of whom are incredibly bright.

Once a week, Jennifer drove into town to have lunch with Dawn. She mentored her throughout middle school and high school, giving her what she needed most—love and time. Throughout the years, Jennifer continued to reach out to her on a weekly basis, and the two grew close.

At the time of this writing, Dawn is twenty-two years old and is practically a part of our family. She loves our children, and our children love her. She comes over for visits and spends time with us. Part of the deal with this mentoring program was that you could not provide a college scholarship for the student you were mentoring. So instead of providing a scholarship for Dawn, we provided one for her sister.

However, we still helped Dawn by guiding her through her studies and helping with some of her living expenses as she finished her bachelor's degree. She recently graduated and is now preparing to pursue a master's degree in occupational therapy.

Again, generosity connected us in a way no one or nothing else could have. Now, any life Dawn and her sister touch through their life's work, we have the privilege of playing a small part in.

The key to finding joy in generosity is giving as if you're giving directly to God. When you give to Him, He gives back even more. The more you bless, the more He blesses. You'll never be able to out-give Him, but if you try, you'll be amazed at how He takes care of you.

Right Place, Right Time

I woke up early for a flight to Botswana one morning to a very disappointed look on Jennifer's face.

"What's the matter?" I asked her.

"Our travel agent just called. We have to stay two nights in Johannesburg on the way to Botswana," she replied.

I dreaded it immediately. I'd been there before, and it wasn't my favorite place to stay, especially overnight. The area is rough, not a place you want to vacation for a few days, especially while trying to relax. But we determined to make the best of it.

One night, we had dinner at a rooftop restaurant overlooking the city. It was beautiful. Our waiter was a friendly young man named Teddy. He liked to talk, so naturally, he and my wife struck up a conversation. We found out that he was not supposed to be working that night, but his boss had called him in unexpectedly.

He asked about our trip, and we told him how much we loved Botswana and how the people we met there meant so much to us. I told him about our mission work and about my son Curtis who trained doctors to go into the villages and take care of the people. At that point, tears began streaming down his face. He tried to hold them back, but it was no use.

"That's what I wanted to do," he whispered through the tears.

Finally, he collected himself and began to tell us his story. Teddy's parents were murdered several years before, and he had moved to Johannesburg as a refugee. He had gotten a job at the hotel with hopes to save enough money to move back to Congo and enter medical school. He knew it would take a while, but he wanted to become a doctor so that he could take care of others who are less fortunate.

Jennifer and I believed that God had brought us to Teddy. Here we were, in a city we were not supposed to be in, on a day we were not supposed to be there, with a waiter who was not supposed to be working, who had lived his whole life with a life dream similar to our son's. We were in the right place at the right time.

Right now, Teddy is in his second year of medical school in Pretoria, South Africa. We have the privilege of funding his education and watching him pursue his purpose. Again, generosity is the thread that connects our hearts, and it will touch many more to come through him.

The same thing happened when we went to visit Jerry and Jana later that week. Jerry met us one morning at the place we were staying, the Royal Tree Lodge, so that we could talk about upcoming projects. While we were there, Jerry told us that he didn't even realize that the lodge, a beautiful four-star game farm on five hundred acres of land, had even existed, although it was only fifteen miles from the mission.

The acreage boasts almost all the wildlife that can be found throughout the region. The only ones missing (for safety reasons) are elephants and predators. I thought it was amazing that we could watch the wildlife right outside the lodge. The owner was nearby and must have overheard our conversation about how incredibly stunning we thought it was.

He asked Jerry, "It's for sale. Do you want to buy it?"

Jerry acted a little embarrassed and later told me he was thinking, "I'm a missionary! How on earth could I possibly buy that?"

But in my heart, I felt that maybe God was up to something. I didn't bring it up until a couple of months later.

I called Jerry and asked him to check on the details of the lodge. He got the information for me, thinking I wanted to buy it for myself. But I realized that as quickly as his nonprofit organization was growing, he needed a for-profit business to keep the income flowing.

One day, I finally let him in on my plan.

"Jerry, I want to buy this lodge to help with the expenses of the mission," I said.

He was in shock. I negotiated a deal, and we bought it at a decent price. Now, the four-star, twenty-four-bed luxury safari lodge and game preserve is owned by Love Botswana. It has hosted several known figures such as Steve Coogan from the popular show, *The Amazing Race*, Joe Jonas of the Jonas Brothers, and both the president and vice president of Botswana. It serves as one of the largest income streams for the outreach programs of Love Botswana. Today, Love Botswana is the largest nongovernmental, nonprofit organization in the entire country.

God will cause you to be in the right place at the right time. You've just got to move when He says. When we sold the business, had we waited even three months later, we would've sold it for considerably less than the amount that we received. We move when we feel Him placing a passion in our hearts for something or someone. When we feel that passion, we know it's time for action.

The Royal Tree Lodge, 2014

When you are used to working on the business side of things, you'll quickly find that not everyone involved in mission work is quite as business-minded as you are. That's okay; they aren't all made to be. That's where we come in. Whenever I work with others, I constantly remind them that the Scripture says that before you build, you should count the cost.[10]

> ### In Their Words
>
> *Rein is a strategic giver. He counts the cost and looks at the capacity of the recipient to be able to manage the investment. He is "hands on" in his approach, visiting often and enjoys watching the progress, even if the progress is slow due to the fact of building in a remote African region. (Jana Lackey, Love Botswana)*

God will entrust more as we prove we are capable of handling what He has already given us. When we're faithful with the little, we're given more. More responsibility, more resources, and more influence. **God always blesses people He knows He can trust to use their wealth to honor Him.**

---

[10] Luke 14:28

It's Not Over

I'm a firm believer in the idea that the minute your soul passes into eternity is the minute you're to be done working here on earth. Until my time comes, I am going to do everything I can to further the Kingdom of God.

One of the ways we are doing this now is by investing in a company in Maun, Botswana. Through our investment, we are allowing the company to operate, expand, and employ a lot of local people in their plant. Another way is through our recently founded Familie Capital Group. This is a family company we designed with the children in mind. For one, it will help them financially, but it will also hopefully keep them together long after we are gone.

Each one of the children put some money into this group and together invested into a startup with the pharmaceutical technology developed by Tulane University. This startup is working with the government to find a cure for several autoimmune disorders, and it looks promising. If the project succeeds, it will be a great help in dealing with outbreaks of epidemic proportions for flu and other common viruses.

The next project we are working on is a bit more involved. As we put the final touches on the Life Center, we realized that it would be the last of our major Love Botswana projects for a while.

This isn't because we wanted to stop helping them but because we had put enough on their plate to utilize for now. And they are utilizing all of it well. The last time we were there, it was such a joy to see the Life Center in action. It was like a busy little hub right in the middle of Northwest Botswana, with meetings, dance recitals, music lessons, and all kinds of other things going on.

Although we felt God was leading us to give Jerry and Jana a break from new projects, we didn't feel like our mission work was done completely. So again we prayed and asked God to make our paths clear.

As we continued to seek Him about our next big project, I made arrangements for Jennifer and me to accompany my sister Sigi and her husband David on their yearly journey through South Africa. Because they had lived there for ten years before, they had a few connections in the area and were invited to speak in several churches that trip. I thought this would be a good chance for Jennifer and me to check up on my sister, as well as to hear her speak.

Our plans were to meet Sigi and David in Capetown and to visit a few churches around there. Next, we would drive the Garden Route and then on to Botswana so that Sigi could speak at Love Botswana's yearly camp meeting. However, a few days before the trip, Jerry called to let us know that he had to switch the dates of the meeting. Because of the modification, our destination was completely changed.

The Miracle of East London

We ended up flying into the other side of Africa and driving up to East London earlier than we had planned, stopping at a cute, quaint bed-and-breakfast called the White House. We got to know the owners and realized that they were believers, which was not uncommon for this part of the country.

On Sunday, we were invited to a church located right in the heart of downtown. It had two services, so the idea was that I would preach in the first service and Sigi in the second. Early that morning, we got dressed and made our way to the church. We spoke with the ministers there and found them to be extremely nice and well-educated people. After brief introductions and a prayer, we entered the sanctuary together.

I looked around, and the sight was unreal. The building sat about four hundred people, but there were many more in there. There were chairs in the aisles, the overflow rooms were spilling out with people, the doors to the outside were open, and people were flooding the entryways and the stairs. The people were so hungry to hear the Word of God. It was beautiful.

I also noticed that there were a lot of students in there, which made sense, since there were colleges all throughout the area. On top of that, most of these people didn't have cars, so they lived downtown and needed to attend somewhere within walking distance.

There was an abortion clinic right across the street that they ministered in as well as a camp they worked with located in a nearby township with over one hundred thousand people residing in it.

There was no question; this church was making an impact in its community.

After a couple of songs were sung, the pastor got up to address the congregation. She spoke of a building program that they were in to increase the size of the church building.

If ever there was a place that needed it, this would be it, I thought to myself as I looked around once more.

It was obvious that the people there were not wealthy, but their hearts for their church and community showed when it was time to bring up their offerings. By the end of the pastor's talk, glass jars and plastic cans filled with change lined the stage. This touched my heart so deeply. The love that these people had for God, for His house, and for their community was astounding.

Both of the services went well, but afterward, I couldn't get the picture of those jars of change out of my mind. I knew their gifts, though given generously, weren't nearly enough, so I wondered what their plan was. I approached the pastor and asked her to explain more.

"This is a poor area, but we are doing our best. The problem is that because of the inflation here, any money we raise this year won't be enough next year," she said matter-of-factly. "We just continue because we trust that God wants this. So we know He will take care of us."

What faith! I thought.

On the ride home, I could feel my heart being challenged. Was this to be our next project? I casted a quick glance at Jennifer and could tell that she too was thinking it over. When we got back to the bed-and-breakfast, we talked about it.

"What do you think?" I asked.

"I think we need to do what we always do," she responded. "Let's take some time and pray."

So we did. Just a short time earlier, we had decided to place both of our homes in North Carolina on the market—the home we lived in and our guest home. As we prayed, we decided that we wouldn't use the foundation money; but if one of our houses sold, we would send the money to the East London church. Hardly any time went by when the house we lived in sold. So we kept our word. We wrote a check for the amount down to the very last penny and sent it to the church.

A few months later, we went back to East London and met with an architect. He was shocked that someone who wasn't even a resident of the area would give such a large sum of money to help them. We had plans drawn up for a building that fit their style—one that used a lot of bricks. It advanced their ministry at least ten years.

Foundation Stone for the Downtown Christian Center, East London, South Africa, 2014

This building will be the first big building built in a long time. Because of its historical value as a German Baptist Church built in 1957, the church cannot be torn down. Instead, they will build over and around it. The church owns a couple of small houses beside the building that they can tear down and build in place of to increase the size of main building.

We are in the midst of the building program right now, and we couldn't be more excited about it. At the time of this writing, we are preparing to make a trip to East London to be there as they lay the cornerstone of the building. Then we will take another trip for the first service in the new building, which is set for November of 2015. Finally, we will return for the official opening in March of 2016, where the city officials will speak and bless the building.

Who would have thought that a change in our itinerary would lead us to our next project? Who would have thought that our house would sell so quickly? In our minds, this is most definitely what we call a God thing. And we couldn't be more thrilled about it.

Our goal has always been and will always be to follow Christ's leading, to affect as many people as possible with the gifts we give. We want to be efficient, to do the most we can with what we've been blessed with. And part of that is joining forces with the Downtown Christian Center.

With Sigi and Jennifer at the Downtown Christian Center in East London, South Africa, 2014

External and internal plan for the new Downtown Christian Center building in East London, South Africa

AFTERWORD

Legacy: Living a Life Worth Leaving

Saying good-bye to everyone in Botswana was tough, especially the children. Now as we board our flight home, I know those little faces will forever be etched into my memory. I can hardly wait to visit them again, although I know it will be nearly six months before I can.

Thankfully, I have my own little ones to go home to. The thought of getting home excites me now because I know my own grandchildren will be waiting for me, yelling "Opa" and will be asking to hear my stories as soon as we walk through the door.

It excites me because, although part of my purpose is to impact the lives of these children, there's another part to my legacy, one that is so incredibly dear to my heart. It's the legacy I leave for my family–for my children and grandchildren.

See, I want to make my life count–for them, for their children, and for their children's children. I want the inheritance I leave to be more than just a monetary one. I want to leave a legacy of faith, courage, humility, and unconditional love. If there's one thing I've learned the last fifty plus years, it's that being a parent or grandparent is not an easy job, but it is, in my opinion, my most important role.

It was December of 1970. The sharp ring pierced through the cold night air.

No one ever calls me at this time of night, I thought to myself. It must be serious.

I made my way to the phone and picked it up, hearing a soft, somber voice on the other line.

"Hi, Rein," the voice said. It took me a second to recognize it. It was my mother.

"Mother? How are you? Is everything all right?" I asked, still trying to wake up. There was a pause, followed by a sigh.

"It's your father. He . . . he passed away, Rein. He's gone."

In that moment, I was sure my heart stopped beating. I mean, Dad wasn't exactly young, but he was healthy. He had recently had a case of bronchitis, but it was nothing serious. He had gone into the hospital to make sure everything was okay. During visiting hour, Mom and Sigi went into see him. While they were there, he had a heart attack and passed away. None of us were expecting him to go so soon. He was only sixty-nine.

I hung up the phone and booked my flight for the next morning to Hanover, where Dad and Mother had been living since they had moved to West Germany from East Berlin. As I sat in my home office chair, thinking back on my childhood, I began to cry. I knew that the tears came, partly because of the sadness of losing my father but also partly because I never really got to tell him how much his life had impacted mine. I would forever be grateful for the legacy he had left behind.

I'm sure there were times Dad wished he had a financial legacy to leave for us, but the governments and systems put in place during his time ensured that he wouldn't have one. Still, Dad's legacy far surpassed any monetary inheritance. He was the kind of man I wanted to be like. He taught me to ask, "What really matters?" and to pursue that with all my heart.

So that's what I do. Every day, I strive to pursue a life that counts, to leave behind a legacy that my children, grandchildren, and great-children will be proud to be a part of.

Saying Good-bye Again

Mother was twelve years younger than Dad, so after his death, she lived alone in Germany for quite a while. Thankfully, Christel lived close to her there, so she had some company but never wanted to remarry. She said that she was not interested in looking after a man again, but I know that the truth was that her heart still was and always would be Dad's.

During the time following Dad's death, Jennifer and I had our hands full in Canada with Chemcraft. However, I went to Germany and Denmark two to three times a year on business, so I always made it a point to be with Mom while there as much as possible.

About ten years after Dad's passing, I got a call from one of my sisters saying that Mother was not doing well, so Jennifer and I flew to Germany to visit her. As we spent time with her, she kept complaining about things disappearing from her apartment. We realized that she was suffering from some type of memory loss–related problem. It was tough to see my once-strong mother now so confused and helpless. We weren't sure what the issue was, but we decided we would help in any way we could.

We took her to one of the best geriatric doctors in the area. When we went in for her appointment, the doctor asked her all kinds of current event–related questions, such as who the president of the United States was and who the prime minister of Germany was. Of course, she knew the answers to those questions because she watched television all day! He told us that nothing was wrong, and we were so embarrassed. He thought we were just trying to get rid of her! But later, she was diagnosed with dementia, which of course was a sad thing, but it gave us more understanding of what was happening.

Because Sigi and I were both living in the States by this time, we moved Mother over as well. First, she lived with Sigi, and then we put her in a nursing home close to where Sigi lived, in South Central Florida. She lived there two or three years, and Jennifer and I drove down as often as possible to see her.

On one trip in 1997, we stopped by to see her on our way to catch a cruise ship in Key West. We had booked a weeklong cruise, but once we saw that her health was failing, we weren't so sure we wanted to take the trip.

After some urging from my sisters, we decided to go. We had a great trip, but as we docked in Key West a week later, we received the sad news that Mother had passed. About two years later, in 1999, I also got news that my sister Ursula had passed away in Germany because of some type of cancer in her blood. She had needed chemo, but there was none available in Germany. She was still young, so it was quite a heavy loss.

It's in these moments of grief that you're reminded to be grateful for the moments that you have with family because one day, those moments will be gone, and all you'll have left is memories. **Today, I live each day with a goal: to make those moments into memories worth leaving behind.**

In Their Words

Family is very high on Rein's priority list. He used to tell me that God was first, and then it was family, health, and work. He loves playing with his grandkids, and his grandkids love visiting with him. He likes to tell stories about when he was little and jokes around with them a lot. Because he is very stern naturally, it's funny to see him transform into "Opa." My daughter loves to crawl up and sit on his lap. They have a good time with him. (Erin Lee, daughter)

With Sigi and Christel, 2010

The Most Important Job

I had a fairly successful professional life, with plenty of jobs that gave me titles to be proud of. But there's one that trumps them all, and it's Dad. (There's one that comes in close second, though, and it's Opa!) My role in the lives of Marc, Krista, Erin, Austin, Quentin, and Curtis is the most important one to me.

When we first had Marc, I was extremely excited but definitely unaware of the responsibility that came with raising a child. It's a constant balance of love and discipline, and as they grow older, a balance of control and of letting go.

As the kids have gotten older and ventured out of my home, I have found peace in Proverbs 22:6. It says that if you train a child in the way he should go, when he is old, he won't depart from it. Parents are the example children look to first and foremost. **What we instill in our children today will affect their futures for years to come.**

Years ago, I determined that my bosses, colleagues, and friends can have a great view of me; but if my children don't, then I know that I am not fully fulfilling my purpose. I have certainly not been a perfect parent, but that's not what it's about. If I'm not a good example to them in the way I act, I will always try to be a good example in the way I handle myself after the fact. Even at eighty years old, I am striving to leave behind a legacy of faith, courage, humility, perseverance, and unconditional love.

Marc and his two children, Gage and Cheyenne, 2014

**Krista, her husband Chris, and their four children,
Kristen, Tyler, Justin, and Emily, 2014**

**Quentin, his wife Yvette, and their three children,
Summer, Jackson, and Jonathan, 2011**

Austin, his wife Ann Marie, and their two children, Luke and Savannah, 2010

Erin, her husband Michael, and their two children, William and Jenna, 2014

Dr. Curtis, his wife Dana, and their son Gabe, 2014

Faith

The main part of my legacy I hope my children cling onto is the faith I have in God. It is the most important part of my life, and I hope that it always remains the most important part of theirs as well. I pray that they have a deep, personal faith not only in God but also in themselves and in what they can do. I want them to see the greatness they possess and to have confidence that they can make their dreams realities if they will pursue them with passion and persistence.

> ### In Their Words
>
> *Dad has always had faith. His faith has affected mine both as a young person and as an adult. It has blossomed even more since his retirement. His focus has switched from the day-to-day of work to the difference he can make in Botswana and in the other places he works. That's kind of his and Jennifer's core now—looking beyond themselves. The foundation he has built was built to help us live out our faith and become more generous. He emphasizes that it's not his money anyways; it's God's on loan to Him. (Curtis Preik, son)*

Courage

If there's one thing I've learned from owning a company, it's that faith in what you can do is not much without the courage to step out and be bold. You can have confidence in yourself and in your dreams, but until you are brave enough to put in the work to make them happen, you'll remain in a place of mediocrity and, most likely, frustration.

Even though it often takes one initial step, **courage isn't just a one-time thing. It's consistent.** It's waking up every day and working as hard as you can to reach your goals. It's not letting failure become final. It's getting back up every single time you fall, with an even greater will to win than you had before.

> **In Their Words**
>
> *Rein has had many tough seasons in his life, but I know that his example of courage has been a testimony to his kids. So few families are successful, but I can see that when their family gathers, they are living in the light of his legacy. God used all his hurts to make his roots deep, and when our roots are deep, then our lives can overflow with thankfulness. (Sigi Oblander, sister)*

Humility

Another characteristic that I hope my children choose is one that is not so popular today. In our celebrity-crazed culture, it has taken a backseat. But still, it's one of the most important to living a satisfied life, one content on the inside and outside. It's humility.

We all want to "make it," to be someone special, someone unique and extraordinary. We want to be different from everyone else when in reality we are all the same. Sure, we have our unique personalities and appearances, but we all are born, live, and die just the same.

It's a good thing to want to make a unique mark, but never let that keep you from being grateful for the life you live now. There's something to be said for enjoying where you are, for remaining humble in your circumstances, no matter what.

> ### In Their Words
>
> *My first husband was a mechanic. His hands were always rough, dirty, and greasy. I'll never forget my father driving up to our house in his fancy car and walking inside in his fancy suit. I thought, "Oh no. What is he going to think?" But then he walked right up to my husband and shook his hand. That's the kind of man that he is. He's not vain, arrogant, or rude. He treats the everyday man the same as the rich man. He is not your typical wealthy individual. He separates his wealth from who he is. With him, what you have does not determine what you are. (Krista Preik, daughter)*

In the Bible, there's a story about a potter and his clay. The potter molds the clay into a pot. The point is made that everyone wants to be the potter, the one with the honor. No one wants to be the pot that has been molded to serve people. Isn't that a great reflection of the majority of society today? We always want the best positions. If we're at a company, we want to become the president. If we're at church, we want to be on the stage, not back in the kitchen.

But what's so bad about being the pot in this story? It has a very important purpose for which it was specifically shaped. And so do you. In your life, you have had certain experiences, you've developed certain skills, and you've built certain relationships that help you become just who you were created to be. So walk in humility, not comparing yourself or your purpose to anyone else's. Live your life. You're the only one who can.

You might think your purpose is "ordinary." But where would we be without what we view as "ordinary?" Where would we be about the "ordinary" person who touches lives every week by greeting people as they walk into church? What about the "ordinary" person who raises five amazing children? What about the "ordinary" person who teaches them? Can you imagine a life without "the ordinary?"

> ### In Their Words
>
> *Humble is a great word to describe Rein. He doesn't want to be in the limelight or want to be seen. And at the same time, he is an incredibly generous man with the resources that God has placed in his hands. He is humble and generous, and when you can have both of those, it's gold. (Pastor Darryl Bellar, pastor of Journey Church)*

Persistence

I've always been big on physical exercise. One of my favorite things to do is run. It clears your mind and releases endorphins. But most importantly, it teaches you discipline and persistence. I am eighty now and am in good health, and I know it is partly a result of establishing that discipline in my life at an early age.

Discipline in running taught me discipline in life. To fully fulfill our purposes, we have to be disciplined to do what it takes each and every day, no matter how mundane the tasks might seem. From my life, I hope that my children and grandchildren see that **a focused life can turn a little talent into amazing success. The key isn't luck; it's discipline.**

On a run in Banff, 2000

> ## In Their Words
>
> *Dad taught me discipline by teaching me how to run and by never letting me win. From eighth grade on, I could never beat him. Even as an adult, I would run up the steep hill at his home in North Carolina. I think he was seventy years old before I beat him, and he was in so much pain the next day. He pushed himself so hard it was insane! "Slacking off" is not part of his vocabulary.*
>
> *His tenacity is more than being competitive; it's him teaching me to never give up in any endeavor of mine no matter how hard or challenging it is. That has pushed me through a lot in my personal life. He always pushed me to not give up. I have passed that on to my kids, and now they can out run me. (Krista Preik, daughter)*

Unconditional Love

Unconditional love is the most beautiful gift. It's the kind of love God has for us, and it's the kind He wants us to have for each other. There's no better way to discover this type of love than to become a parent. Parenting will test your patience like nothing else, but at the end of the day, you know you love that child more than anything in the world.

We show unconditional love by caring more about who our children are than about what they do. They must know that they are loved because they are *ours*, and there's *nothing* they can do to mess that up.

My parents were the perfect example of unconditional love. They went through so much together, yet they still had one of those envious marriages, the ones that you grow up hoping and dreaming about. They parented us with that same type of love. I know that whether I had been successful in my business pursuits or not, they would have been just as proud, and that meant the world to me. I learned unconditional love from them, and I hope to pass that same love onto my children.

> ### In Their Words
>
> *I admire Rein greatly. Stepparents can go either way. You can have a negative or a positive experience. I'm so thankful that mine has been positive. I genuinely appreciate the role he has played in my life. He is very loyal and loving. He has seen me at my worst and at my best, and he still loves me. He shows love by passing on his wisdom and motivating all of us to do better and to be better. (Erin Lee, daughter)*

Looking back on my life now, I am amazed—amazed at the faithfulness of God and at how I have gotten to where I am. But I know that there are even greater days ahead, for me, for my family, and for our work, investing into lives around the world. I feel honored to have lived this life I have been given. My only hope is that it would now inspire you to live a life that matters. My prayer is that you live each day to leave a legacy.

Top Ten Things You Need to Know About Rein
By the Preik children

10. If Rein says to be ready to leave by 5 p.m., be ready to leave by 4:30 p.m.

9. Rein often confuses the word *hike* with *forced march*.

8. 2 o'clock in the afternoon is coffee and sweets; 4 o'clock in the afternoon is wine and cheese.

7. If you are out for dinner with Rein and he asks you if you want dessert, what he is really asking you is "Please order dessert, so I can order some too."

6. If you are going on a road trip with Rein, be prepared to leave by 4 a.m.—er . . . I mean 3:30 a.m.

5. While on a road trip with Rein, hope and pray that there is a Cracker Barrel on your route, or you might have to stop at a Huddle House.
(But there is an upside; he has a plan. I have it on good authority that he may claim to be a health inspector when entering such a place.)

4. If Rein asks you if you have seen his new car—you probably haven't.

3. Rein's love for his dogs has grown steadily. The first boxer, Coco, was not allowed on the furniture.

Now, if you want to sit down and Mona Lisa got there first—sorry, you're out of luck.

2. By the time you have woken up in the morning, Rein has already walked the dog five miles, washed his car, read his Bible, and is now ready for some lunch.

1. If there is a need to be met and Rein can help out, he will.

Printed in the United States
By Bookmasters